OUT OF THE LIPS OF INFANTS, WISDOM COMES

Retelling The Bible Stories

Adaku Helen Ogbuji, CCVI, Ph.D

En Route Books and Media, LLC
Saint Louis, MO

⊕ENROUTE
Make the time

En Route Books and Media, LLC
5705 Rhodes Avenue
St. Louis, MO 63109

Contact us at **contact@enroutebooksandmedia.com**

Cover Credit: Sr. Adaku Helen Ogbuji

© 2021 and 2023 Adaku Helen Ogbuji, CCVI, Ph.D

ISBN: 979-8-88870-083-9
Library of Congress Control Number: 2023944910

Originally Published by
Franciscan Kolbe Press,
P.O. Box 468, 00217 Kenya

Dedication

This Book is dedicated to all those who love the Word of God and to my friend St. Thérèse of Lisieux (The Little Flower). Her "Little Way,"— the way of spiritual childhood, the way of trust, and absolute surrender, deeply inspired me.

Table of Contents

Acknowledgments iii

Foreword v

Preface ix

Introduction 1

SECTION ONE

Reflections on Selected Passages from Scripture 7

Ch. 1: Rebekah's Role: A Deceit or a Blessings? 9
Ch. 2: Praying the Imprecatory Psalms: A Challenge! 19
Ch. 3: Fuflfilling a Vow Made to God 33
Ch. 4: Mary of Bethany: A Model in Patriarchal Societies. 47
Ch. 5: Freeing a Daughter of Abraham 65
Ch. 6: The Basis of Courage in the Midst of Little Faith 79
Ch. 7: Reclaiming One's Place at the Table 95
Ch. 8: The Impartiality of God: A Pauline Emphasis in
      Romans 2:12-24 113

SECTION TWO

Short Reflections on Biblical Themes...............................133

Ch. 9: An Invitation to a Spiritual Cleansing 135

Ch.10: Remain in My Love..141

Ch. 11: God Shows no Partiality..149

Ch. 12: A Call to Sing Alleluia Even in the Midst of

    Trials: A Reflection on a Shrove Tuesday....................153

Ch. 13: Leaders are Servants 157

Ch. 14: Patience is Very Rewarding.......................................161

Ch. 15: Seeking the Lord at the Well of Our Souls 165

Ch. 16: The Voice of Acceptance! 171

Ch. 17: The Voice of Wrath: Amos and the Corrupt

    Leaders 175

Ch. 18: Do You Want to Be Healers?.....................................181

Ch. 19: Gratitude is the Best Attitude 187

Ch. 20: Compassion: The Only Word the Deaf can Hear.193

Ch. 21: Who do People Say that You Are?............................199

Ch. 22: Recognizing the Voice of the Good Shepherd......205

Conclusion 211

Epilogue...215

References..217

Acknowledgments

I am grateful to God who accomplishes his work through mere infants.

I thank the members of the Catholic Biblical Instructors Union (CBIU), Nigeria. It is through this Society that I started learning how to listen and share the Word of God with my parishioners, from my teenage years.

I thank the Leadership Team and all the Sisters of Charity of the Incarnate Word, Houston for their unwavering support and love.

I appreciate the encouragement and the ceaseless support that I received from my Bishop, Most Rev. Dr. Lucius I Ugorji. Thank you!

I am indebted to my professors at Aquinas Institute of Theology, St. Louis, Missouri, USA who sharpened my skills in theological and scriptural reflection: Fr. Dr. Dan Harris (of blessed memory), Fr. Dr. George Boudreau, Fr. Dr. Don Goergen, Fr. Dr. Seán Charles Martin, Fr. Dr. Richard Peddicord, Sr. Dr. Carla Mae Streeter, Sr. Dr. Colleen Mallon, Sr. Dr. Mary Margaret Pazdan, Dr. Carolyn Wright, and Dr. Ann Garido.

My mum Fidelia Lucy Ogbuji, as a CBIU member, inspired me; so I profoundly thank her. I thank God for the love of my late father, Dee Joe. Fr. Udo, my elder brother is a great homilist and a good story teller. He truly motivated me and helped me with my homiletics class. I am indebted to him for making some recommendations that fine-tuned this book and for writing the foreword. I am grateful to all my younger siblings who love me unconditionally—Gloria, Henry and Prisca. My niece and nephews are wonderful—Amarachi,

Chigozie Joe, Akachukwu, Enyioma, Chimdike Joe, and Gerald Kamsi—I appreciate their love.

I express my sincere gratitude to all my friends who edited this work and supported me—Ms. Melinda Brown, Sr. Ethel Puno, Katherine Leyva, Rev. Dr. Patrick Thawale, for editing and writing the preface, Fr. Dr. Remigius Ikpe, Dr. Austin Igbuku, Sir. Pius Ogiji, Fr. Dr. Emmanuel Foro, Fr. Dr. Reginald Temu, and Sr. Dr. Ngozi Okpalaenwe.

Those I have not mentioned here are dear to me, too. I thank God for the gift you are to me!

Foreword

As kids, we grew up watching our single mother struggle, after the death of her beloved husband and our father, to cater for our needs. We didn't always have what we needed as we faced the hazards of life. However, with every successful milestone and even through misfortune, we learned quickly that our chances of surviving were intrinsically linked to our sticking together as a team, bound by trust and love. In other words, the well-being of each of us depended on us playing our parts as well as on the support we give ourselves.

On a certain day, my sister Helena and I had gone to harvest cassava from my mom's peasant farm. I was 14 years old and she was 10 at the time. Cassava is a root crop and requires enormous strength to pull it out of the ground, so being the stronger one that job fell to me. I mistakenly thought that the dry, clay soil, was my only challenge, but I was wrong. I was unaware that hanging directly above my newly shaved head were clusters of fully ripped, dry agbara beans, hiding in plain sight. For those of you who are not familiar with this type of bean, let me enlighten you. Agbara, as we call it, have tiny hair-like thorns that sting more than the bite of fire ants when they come into contact with human skin. I leaned forward and pulled the cassava tuber from the soil. Upon standing, my sweaty, bald head accidentally slammed into the dreaded agbara beans. The excruciating pain was over-whelming! It felt like I was stung by more than a hundred wasps. Oblivious of what hit me, I fell to the ground like a lunatic and started smearing my head with the dry clay dirt. The pain was unbearable!

At that moment, Helena rushed to my side. Her genuine empathy comforted me tremendously. She looked at my head and told me I would be okay. Her words soothed me and helped me calm down. I didn't realize, at the time, that it took every ounce of self-control for her not to dissolve into laughter at my predicament. However, many years later, she recounted on how she would laugh to her heart's content when out of my sight and then kept a straight face while caring for me without giving any clue that my misery appeared entertaining. Currently, as we recount the story, we laughed together at the hilarious image of a young, crazy lunatic with smeared dirt all over his head.

Helena was a thoughtful, kind child, who knew the right things to say and do at the proper time. Her life as a young girl was a reflection of the gospel in many good ways. You can understand from the story that it would have been hard for anyone not to laugh at my odd predicament. But she didn't make light of my agony, at least not to my face. She really cared! She exercised good judgment and discretion by taking my plight seriously and showed empathy in spite of my jester-like behavior. Even at that young age, she displayed rare wisdom—genuine humanity—and was able to interpret and live the word of God in the moment.

I therefore have no doubt that if anyone can convincingly tell the story of human salvation through the eyes of a babe, it's her. In this book, she did it in a simple, clear, practical and powerful way. I'm sure that you'll find her perspective refreshing and inspiring. She convinced me that I was okay when my head felt like it was on fire. Give her the chance to bring you a clearer understanding of God, and in the process improve your relationship with Him. I therefore recommend this book and masterpiece to you.

Fr. Udochukwu Vincent Ogbuji,
Author of *The Peace I Know*

Preface

In Mt 11: 25-25, Jesus thanks God for revealing these things to mere children. The innocence, wisdom, and sincere mind of children are incredible. Just as they have with their caregivers, kids are open to kindness, forgiveness, reconciliation and they have the inclination to human relationships based on love and decency. Some of the qualities we learn from children are: Wisdom, openness, sincerity, simplicity of heart, forgiveness, and believing and telling it the way it is. These young minds depend on their caregivers totally and they mirror how we are called to completely depend and trust in God, especially at this time when the whole world is battling with COVID—19.

As children of God, we are called to approach the Bible with genuine, child-like openness and with rudimentary curiosity to learn about God and have a relationship with Him. It is this view that Sr. Adaku explicates so beautifully in this book. Approaching the Bible from the point of view of children makes such a big difference. As we all know, the Bible cannot be fully exhausted in its width and depth. It is a living book and it keeps on challenging us. As such, the manner in which children view the Bible is one of the views that adds value to understanding the Bible.

Children think differently from adults. In their child-like approach, they appear naïve, but on the other hand, they are wise and sincere in their thoughts. Sr. Adaku stipulates that she is not writing with proficiency, however, she hopes that the reader would be led to faith in Jesus Christ. The Biblical stories enjoy special liking by children. No wonder the author, talking about her childhood experiences with the Bible, tells us that the Bible meant a lot to her. She indicated that this book is a fruit of her years of learning how to reflect on the Word of God as a child and as an adult. She has, in a skillful manner, presented how each stage of learning, interpretation, interaction and knowledge initiates a fuller understanding of and relationship with God. The manner in which the author presents the theme of the book, through the various twenty two chapters, is so telling of the importance of the book.

The author's reflection has a methodology that stresses on a particular idea accompanied by her experience of the central idea. She rightly suggests that "it is important for the preachers to have a focus or a main idea, or even their own experience of the central idea when they are breaking the Word of God to the congregation. This helps the preacher to be focused. On the part of the listeners, it helps them to get the message clearly and hopefully bring them to faith in Jesus Christ."

The way she has written this book is so inspiring because it helps the reader understand the Word of God in a deeper way. Since Jesus finds it fitting to share his wisdom with mere infants (Mt. 11:25), in the same way, Sr. Adaku demonstrates that wisdom can come from children since Jesus shared it with them. I congratulate her on a job well done.

My hope and prayer is that this book will help readers understand the Word of God and consequently bring them to faith in the

Lord Jesus Christ. May God's blessings and graces accompany the further fruits of this masterpiece.

Rev. Dr. Patrick Thawale,
Vicar General, Archdiocese of Lilongwe, Malawi.

Introduction

"O my God, You know that I have never desired but to love You alone. Your Love has gone before me from my childhood, it has grown with my growth, and now it is an abyss, the depths of which I cannot fathom."
—St. Thérèse of Lisieux (*Story of a Soul*)

My eight-year-old nephew, Vincent Akachukwu, is presently at that age when kids begin to soak up knowledge and information. This period has the feel of innocence and fervent curiosity. These young minds are so curious, that their ability to churn up questions is almost infinite. Naturally, my nephew asks a lot of questions! His queries are generally good and easy to answer. Although I have to admit that he sometimes asks questions in an attempt to play pranks on adults, for attention, to show off, or to find out how much you know. However, once in a while he comes up with queries that are hard even for a grown-up to answer.

During my last vacation at my sister's home, Vincent sat across the dining table from me doing his homework, as I ate my lunch. I wondered at his silence but didn't have to wait long before his usual curiosity came to the surface. "Auntie," he called out, trying to get my full attention. "Yes my boy!" I answered smiling. "What is the hardest science and what is the hardest math?" he asked. It didn't matter whether his question was genuine or not, I always view such opportunities as teachable moments. I answered his question in such a way as to provoke his thoughts and maybe overcome any objections. "The hardest science is knowing who you are, and the hardest math is measuring yourself," I responded with a smile. "Of course," he protested, "I know who I am!" "Well then, Who are you?" I asked. He proceeded to tell me his full name. "You're not your name and you know that," I replied. Then Vincent gave another answer: "I'm a person!" he blurted out. I asked him which person he was, the boy who gets into trouble many times a day, or the one who helps out in the kitchen. He admitted to being both boys, good and bad, and was beginning to understand how difficult it is to fully grasp who we are as individuals. After somewhat conceding to the difficulty of knowing oneself with certainty, he said, "It is easy to measure myself." "Are you sure about that?" I asked hoping he'd reconsider. He ignored my cautionary tone, ran to his room, got a tape measure and went to the mirror to measure himself. He came out and proudly announced: "I'm three and a half feet!" I smiled at him, but shook my head.

Vincent was shocked when I shook my head in disagreement. I patiently explained my view by asking him a question, "If you don't have limbs, is it still you?" "Yes, it's me," he responded. "Go ahead then and measure your limbless self," I suggested. He did and came up with two feet. Now there is more to this story which I'll share later in the book. Suffice it to say that this experience with my nephew took me back to myself at his age, and I thought to myself, "Kids are really curious, sincere, intelligent, quick to learn, and always willing to share their wisdom with adults." This understanding moved me to reflect on the Word of God from a "child-like perspective", hoping that it will be a witness to those who seek to read the Scriptures differently through stories, idioms, and parables.

This book title: "Out of the Lips of Infants, Wisdom Comes: Retelling the Bible Stories," was an inspiration from the words of Jesus in Matthew 11:25-26. In this passage, Jesus thanked God for revealing the secret of the kingdom to mere children. The reflections contained in this book are "my infant" ways of reflecting on the scriptural passages. It is told simply, however, it can lead the reader to faith in Jesus Christ. St. Francis exhorts us to preach the Word of God everywhere and if necessary to use words and that is what I started doing at a very tender age.

During my teenage years and early twenties, I was a member of the Catholic Biblical Instructors Union (CBIU), Nigeria. The Union was founded in 1975 by Fr. Benedict I. Nwolu ("Humble Founder," as he was popularly called when he was alive), a diocesan priest from Isialangwa L.G.A., Abia State, Nigeria. This Union is dedicated to studying, reflecting, and sharing the Bible as well as the beliefs, practices, and Doctrines of the Church to its members as well as Catholic lay faithful. All the CBIU members are referred to as "Humble Members" and the branch/parish leaders, "Humble Servants." The CBIU National Council is led by Humblest Servants, while the Provinces/Dioceses are led by Humbler Servants. Studying the Scriptures and the Doctrines of the Church are paramount to the affairs of the Union, since the prospective members would later teach others. It is also important to know that the mottos of the Union are: "No half measures," (Rev. 3:16) and "Actions speak louder than words" (Jas.

1:22; Mt. 7:24; 1 Jn. 3:18). This means that the members are expected to walk the talk as faithful Catholics.

As a "promised member" of CBIU for over fifteen years before I joined religious life, I developed a deep love for the stories in the Bible and I brought them to wherever I was sent by the Union. A "promised member" is one who vows to preach the Word of God, through actions and words, as well as abiding by the rules of the Union. Before one becomes a "promised member," he/she has to be steadfast in Catholic faith and also undergo years of formation and studying the Bible.

During this time, I shared the Word of God with CBIU members and also to my parishioners, mostly before the beginning of Sunday Masses. Each week has a Biblical theme that mirrors the theme of each Sunday's Gospel message. This means that one has to arrive an hour earlier than the actual time of the Mass and ready to catechize the faithful with the Word of God. CBIU and its formation helped me to gain much knowledge about the stories of the Holy Scripture. Similarly, joining Aquinas Institute of Theology, as a graduate student, refined and polished me in various ways of doing Biblical exegesis.

This book is the fruit of my years of learning how to reflect on the Word of God, both as a child and as an adult; and how each stage of learning, interpretation, interaction and knowledge, initiated a fuller understanding of and relationship with God. The work is arranged in two sections. Section one contains the reflections and exegeses from the Hebrew Scriptures and the New Testament, while section two is comprised of short reflections on several themes from

Scripture passages. Chapter one tells the story of Rebekah the wife of Isaac and examines whether Rebekah's manipulation was a deceit or a blessing. Chapters two and three explore the Book of Psalms: while chapter two illuminates the challenges of praying the cursing psalms, chapter three reflects on Psalm 66. Chapter four expounds on the fearless character of Mary of Bethany in John's gospel and how she can be a model for women in patriarchal societies. Chapter five retells the story of Jesus and the Crippled Woman, while chapter six examines Peter's lack of faith and connects it with our own little faith during life's storms. Chapter seven examines the powerful faith of the Canaanite woman as well as Jesus' cultural prejudice. Chapter eight ends section one by explaining the impartiality of God through St. Paul's letter to the Romans.

Section two presents short reflections on several themes from Scriptural passages. Chapter nine invites us to spiritual cleansing through St. Luke's gospel (11:37-41); while chapter ten examines the marriage between a Muslim and a Christian with the Gospel of John 15: 9-12. The theme of this chapter highlights the importance of remaining in Christ's love. Chapter eleven reflects about God's impartiality while chapter twelve calls us to sing Alleluia even in the midst of trials. In chapter thirteen, the need for a servant-leadership was illuminated and chapter fourteen looks at the virtue of patience as rewarding. In chapters fifteen and sixteen the story of the Samaritan woman at the well was retold in two different ways, chapter seventeen declares the wrath of God on corrupt leaders through the prophesy of Amos, while chapter eighteen asks the question: Do you want to be healed? Chapter nineteen explains why gratitude is the

best attitude in our daily living, and chapter twenty reveals that compassion is the only word "the deaf can hear." Exploring the Christological question Jesus asked the disciples, chapter twenty- one asks
us the same question: Who do people say that we are? Finally, chapter twenty-two explains the need to recognize the voice of the Good
Shepherd. The conclusion summarizes the book while the epilogue
creates feelings of optimism, courage, and hope during this COVID-
19 pandemic.

In section two, each chapter has a purpose and a central idea that
is communicated throughout the reflection. It is significant for
preachers to have a focus or a main idea, a purpose and even their
own experience of the central idea when they are sharing the Word
of God with the congregation. Having one central idea keeps the
preacher from wandering away, because there could be several
themes in a particular pericope. It also helps the listeners understand
the message clearly and hopefully builds their faith in Jesus Christ.

It is my hope that this wisdom from the "lips of an infant" will
help the reader understand the Word of God in a simple yet deeper
way, and hopefully bring them to faith in our Lord Jesus Christ. This
reflection is for all those who love the Word of God.

SECTION ONE

REFLECTIONS ON
SELECTED PASSAGES FROM SCRIPTURE

Chapter 1

REBEKAH'S ROLE: A DECEIT OR A BLESSING?
(Gen. 25:19-34; 27-28:1-10)

"There is no artist who does not like his work praised, and the Divine Artist of souls is pleased when we do not stop at the exterior, but penetrate even to the inmost sanctuary where He dwells."

—St. Thérèse of Lisieux (*Story of a Soul*)

The story of Rebekah and her twin children has always intrigued me. I have sometimes wondered whether her special love for Jacob was a betrayal on her part as the mother to her other son Esau, whom she was equally meant to love and care for. As one of the matriarchs of the Jews, was Rebekah making sure that the right son received his father's blessing? (Gen. 25:23) Was Isaac aware of the differences in the character qualities of his sons, and thus went along with Rebekah's plan intentionally? Consider Esau's personality: he sought immediate gratification resulting in selling his birthright for a bowl of stew (Gen. 25:29-34), and married foreigners who made life bitter for Isaac and Rebekah (Gen. 26:34-35). Was the blessing still meant for him?

This reflection is an analysis of the manipulation and diversion of Esau's blessings through Rebekah's strategies. It will also ascertain whether her deceit was a blessing in disguise for the fulfillment of God's plan.

9

The sibling rivalry between Esau and Jacob started when they were in the womb (Gen. 25:22). After twenty years of childlessness (Gen. 25:20, 26), Rebekah was granted the favor of fruitfulness, thanks to Isaac's answered prayer. A midrash sees this answered prayer as "an object lesson in the power of prayer to move God from anger to mercy."[1] Midrash is a Hebrew word which literally means to probe or to examine. It is used by Jewish Scripture scholars (Rabbi) to interpret and examine a particular passage in order to ascertain a deeper meaning that is implied.

As Isaac prayed to be blessed with children, Rebekah did nothing about her barrenness, unlike Hannah who prayed fervently for a child (1 Sam. 1:9-19). On the other hand, Isaac never took a hand-maid like his father Abraham did, when he and Sarah experienced barrenness (Gen. 16:1-4).

After conception, Rebekah was greatly bothered by the violent movements of the children in her womb, and because of this, she even began to question why she was alive (Gen. 25:22). Valerie Lieber noted that this inquiry is often asked when women are having problems with conception, but Rebekah asked this during the pregnancy.[2] This question and the struggles in her womb could have prompted her to seek divine help. The word used in Hebrew for this

---

[1] Jon D. Levenson, "Genesis: Introduction and Annotations," in *The Jewish Study Bible*, ed. Adele Berlin and Marc Z. Brettler (New York, NY: Oxford University Press, 2004), 53.

[2] Valerie Lieber, "Contemporary Reflection," in *The Torah: A Women's Commentary*, 152.

inquiry is lidrosh which means a formal consultation with God.[3] Rebekah interacted with God directly and God responded in kind. During this inquiry, she discovered that she was pregnant with twins and that the older would serve the younger (Gen. 25:23). Was Isaac aware of the answer to the inquiry? In other words, was Isaac aware of his children's divine destiny?

The question now is, who is the older among the twins and why would he serve the younger? Benjamin Goodnick explained in Midrash from Rashi that Jacob was conceived first and Esau second, but because Esau was in the fetal position to be born first, Jacob was deprived of his birthright.[4] The Scriptures tell us that Esau was the older of the twins but he later sold this birthright to Jacob. Selling it meant that he was no longer considered to be the oldest, and he would later despised this birthright (Gen. 25:34). The Hebrew word for birthright is b'chorah. In the Near East in ancient times, the birthright referred to the status given to the firstborn son who would become the successor of the corporate household. The person was entitled to certain economic and religious privileges that came with the position. In Judaism, the son with this status has a special relationship with God. He is set aside as God's possession and considered as quasi-holy.[5]

---

[3] Tamara C. Eskenazi and Hara Person, "Shaping Destiny: The Story of Rebekah," in The Torah: A Women's Commentary, ed. Tamara Eskenazi and Andrea Weiss (New York, NY: Women of Reform Judaism Press, 2008), 136.

[4] Benjamin Goodnick, "Rebekah's Deceit or Isaac's Great Test." The Jewish Bible Quarterly 23, no. 4 (October-December 1995): 222.

[5] Goodnick, 224.

The question still remains: How morally justifiable was the means that Jacob utilized to gain the birthright? The truth is that Jacob's action was morally wrong. His dishonest way of acquiring the birthright would bring many tragedies and trials to his life: Jacob became his brother's enemy; he fled his home out of fear of Esau and never saw his mother again; he was deceived by his uncle Laban; he would lose his beloved wife Rachel and his son Joseph would be sold into slavery; and finally, he would end up in exile in Egypt. With Jacob acquiring the birthright status, he was automatically entitled to receive the blessing of the first born son. Rebekah became the instrument used to successfully execute God's plan for these two brothers.

These twin brothers were distinct from birth, and they followed different lifestyles as well as different historical destinies. Esau lived for the moment and sought after immediate gratification: living as a hunter he was characteristically direct and fast. In ancient Israel, Esau's hunting suggested uncouthness which would manifest itself in impulsive behavior as he exchanged his birthright for food.[6] His personality would be seen in his impatient reactions when he was tired and hungry from hunting. He expressed his tiredness with crude words, such as: "I am famished and about to die" as well as "give me some of that red stuff to gulp down" (Gen. 25:29-32). Goodnick noted that gulping the food rather than eating normally indicates Esau's impatience and uncouthness.[7] The satisfaction of his hunger would cost him his birthright which he would later despise. This trait of self-gratification was possibly inherited from his father Isaac. If

---

[6] Levenson, 53.

[7] Goodnick, 224.

not, what accounts for his desire to have a delicacy before blessing his son? Furthermore, Esau's intermarriages outside of their clan would become a source of bitterness to his parents (Gen. 26:34-35). These marriages contrasted with Abraham's effort to find a wife for Isaac from within their household (Gen. 24:1-9). Jon Levenson explained that these improper marriages of Esau made him unworthy to serve as the next figure in the patriarchal line.[8]

In contrast, Jacob was a quiet man, who stayed home (Gen. 25:27); it enabled learning, studying, and meditating on the knowledge of God. This gave him the advantage over Esau, of carrying on the religious heritage of their ancestors.[9] Jacob was also very patient, disciplined, shrewd, and long suffering. These characteristics were clearly seen in his willingness to serve Laban for fourteen years in exchange for marriage to his two daughters. As a disciplined and long-suffering person, Jacob knew the right time to approach Esau to buy the birthright. He understood that Esau was the kind of man to give anything impulsively for self-gratification. The longing and desire to acquire Esau's status implies that Jacob placed higher value on things that last—possession of the birthright, rather than on self-gratification. Interestingly, the rabbinic literature adorns Jacob with the garments of righteousness and virtue (the tzadik), while Esau is portrayed as wicked (rasha).[10]

---

[8] Levenson, 55.

[9] Plaut, Bamberger, and Hallo, 175.

[10] Pesach Schindler, "Esau and Jacob Revisited: Demon versus Tzadik?" Jewish Bible Quarterly 35, no.3 (2007): 153.

As the twins grew up, the partiality of their parents was noticeable. Isaac loved Esau because he enjoyed the food provided through Esau's hunting. Although Rebekah's love for Jacob was not explained, it could have been influenced by the divine revelation she had received. Thus, her love did not depend on self-gratification (Gen. 25:28). Most likely she was mediating on God's preference: "I have shown you love, said the LORD.... Esau is Jacob's brother; yet I have accepted Jacob and have rejected Esau." (Mal. 1:2-5). This favor of God was also manifest in his choice of Abel over Cain, Isaac over Ishmael, as well as Joseph over his brothers. Goodnick was of the view that perhaps Rebekah became closer to Jacob because he was helpful to her in household chores and maybe he even learned to cook.[11] Conversely, Isaac probably preferred Esau since both were men who worked in the field (Gen. 26:12).

When Isaac was preparing to bless his favorite son Esau, Rebekah overheard his instructions and realized that she needed to act quickly to ensure that the divine oracle would be given to the right person. The manipulative behavior of Rebekah makes one think about the fulfillment of this divine oracle. Does God need the assistance of Rebekah to fulfill this promise? Goodnick suggests that Rebekah did not see her actions as deceptive, rather that she was the instrument through which God would fulfill his promise.[12]

Before bestowing the blessing, Isaac sent Esau out to the field to hunt some game for him; the reason why Esau was his favorite son. Did Isaac really need food before bestowing the blessing? Could it

---

[11] Goodnick, 223.

[12] Goodnick, 225.

have been a strategy to get him out of the house until the blessing had been given to Jacob? As a good homemaker, Rebekah handled the clothing of Jacob as well as the preparation of food for Isaac. Jacob was afraid to take the risk of deceiving his father and the consequence of being cursed by him. Rebekah however convinced Jacob into thinking that she would bear his curse (Gen. 27:12-13). Perhaps her readiness to take full responsibility for a possible curse, pointed to her understanding of the divine oracle, and showed that her deception was not for personal gain.

When Jacob appeared before his father Isaac, he challenged his impersonation six times in Gen. 27:18, 20, 21-22, 24, and 26. Why did Isaac press the issue of Jacob's identity six times? Zucker explains that Isaac probably wants to indoctrinate Jacob and to test him since he is a home-boy whose life has been too easy; and he has remained unmarried even after forty years, while Esau his twin brother already has two wives (Gen. 26:34). It could also mean that Isaac is verifying which of his sons was before him, in order to give the blessing to the one appointed by God.

Isaac challenges Jacob for returning from the hunt so quickly and uses every sense left in him—hearing, tasting, touching, and smelling—to ascertain whether he was blessing the right son. He questions Jacob's voice which had betrayed him. Isaac also tasted his meal. Because Rebekah knew Isaac's favorite meal, she had prepared one that would please her husband. Isaac felt Jacob's hands to see how hairy they were and even smelled his son who was wearing his brother's cloak. At the end of all this drama, Isaac was deceived or probably he allowed the divine oracle to come to fulfillment.

In his response, Jacob makes five false claims: twice affirming that he was Esau, that he had prepared the meal, that he had been asked by his father to hunt the game for the meal, and finally that his success was through divine providence (Gen. 27:19-24). Although Jacob was lying to his father by invoking God's name, this invocation could be a reflection of God's preference for Jacob rather than his father's choice, Esau.

Isaac later blessed Jacob and used the same divine words that Rebekah had received from God when she was pregnant: "Be master over your brothers, and let your mother's sons bow to you" (Gen. 27:29). The words, "sons and brothers," could be references to the future descendants of Esau since Jacob has only one brother.

Some commentators have wondered whether Isaac was truly deceived. Although Isaac had become blind because of old age, his hearing had not failed him. Plaut, et al., believe that Isaac has no doubt about Esau's identity. They think that Isaac was probably not courageous enough to face Esau; thus, he allowed himself to be misled by Jacob. Perhaps he expected that Esau would not carry the covenant of Abraham.[13]

According to David Zucker, Rebekah and Isaac worked mutually to mislead Jacob into thinking that he is stealing the blessing meant for Esau. He believes that it was Jacob who was deceived since the previous dialogue between Esau and his father made it clear that Isaac knew his children well in spite of his blindness.[14] Zucker's

---

[13] Plaut, Bamberger, and Hallo, 190.

[14] David Zucker, "The Deceiver Deceived: Rereading Genesis 27," Jewish Bible Quarterly 39, no.1 (2011): 46-47.

argument is that there is no tension between Isaac and Rebekah and that even when Isaac discovers that he has blessed Jacob, he did not behave like someone who was deceived. He never cursed either his wife or Jacob, rather he blessed Jacob more with the blessing of Abraham (Gen. 28:1-4). Most likely Isaac was not happy that Esau willingly sold his birthright to his younger brother, nor was he pleased that Esau married women outside of their clan (Gen. 26:34-35). Thus, Isaac chose to be blind to what he wished not to see.

When Esau returned from the field, he wept bitterly before his father. Zucker explains that Isaac was seized with violent trembling because his game with Rebekah was a deception on Esau whom he loved. However, Isaac was secretly pleased that the right son got the blessing.[15] The evidence of Isaac's satisfaction that Jacob got the blessing was the occasion of a second blessing when Rebekah expressed her fear that Jacob might marry from outside their clan. This second blessing is even more significant, especially with the invoking of the blessing of Abraham on him and his offspring. It designates Jacob as the successor of the Abrahamic covenant rather than Esau. At this point, Jacob left their home not only fleeing from his brother's wrath, but was also following the family's tradition of finding a wife for himself from his uncle Laban's household (Gen. 28:1-5).

Ultimately, Rebekah is portrayed as the heroine who followed the divine oracle given to her by God in order to maintain the covenantal relationship between her father-in-law Abraham and God. Although it seems as if Rebekah takes the law into her own hands by not allowing the divine oracle to unfold, it could be that God used her as an

---

[15] Zucker, 55.

instrument since God's plan had to be fulfilled somehow. The question to ponder is this: how would the divine oracle have come to fulfillment if Isaac had given Esau the blessing? Indeed, Rebekah intervened to ensure that Isaac did the right thing. Actually, the divine oracle started unfolding when Esau married outside of their clan and his wives made life miserable for both Rebekah and Isaac. No matter how much love Isaac had for Esau, he would not have condoned Esau's foreign wives. Nevertheless, Isaac suffered in silence even as Esau sold his birthright for self-gratification.

With this attitude of Esau, Rebekah, as a wise woman, knows that God's divine oracle is manifesting even before she acts. She and her husband were aware of Esau's uncouthness as well as Jacob's virtuous character. For the fact that when Isaac discovered that he had blessed Jacob, he did not behave like someone who had been deceived; suggests that Isaac knew that Esau was not worthy to continue with Abrahamic covenant. Rather, Isaac blessed Jacob even more with the Abrahamic blessing. Jacob was the chosen son even before he was born. Regardless of the means that Rebekah used, she intervened in order to fulfill the divine oracle revealed to her. Therefore, her manipulation was a disguised blessing.

Chapter 2

PRAYING THE IMPRECATORY PSALMS: A CHALLENGE!

"I ought to seek the company of those who please me least. A word, a kindly smile, will often suffice to gladden a wounded and sorrowful heart."

— St. Thérèse of Lisieux (*Story of a Soul*)

In Cologne Germany during the World War II, this inscription was found on a wall in a cellar where some Jews had hidden from the Nazis: "I believe in the sun, even when it is not shining. I believe in love, even when I cannot feel it. I believe in God, even when He is silent."[1]

The experience of the Holocaust, and the "apparent silence of God," did not deter this anonymous author, who perished with fellow victims, to doubt the existence of God. The author believed in God based on what he/she wrote. In the midst of hard times, many often raise questions about the existence of God: Why is this happening to me? Is God dead? Is God silent? Where is God in the midst of racial hatred, prejudices, discrimination, and bigotry? In ancient Israel, the perceived silence of God, to the cry of the people, is also

---

[1] Douglas Berner, The Silence is Broken! God Hooks Ezekiel's Gog and Magog, (Morrisville, NC: Lulu Press, 2006), 173.

accompanied by a precatory psalm to remind God of His covenant with them.

Psalms are poetic texts or hymns that were used by ancient Israelites in their daily worship of God in the temple, synagogues, homes, work places, as well as on their way to the temple. Also contained in the Book of Psalms are prayers for thanksgiving, praise, lament, forgiveness of sins, protection, favor, vengeance, healing, etc. Some psalms were for instructions or ceremonies, some were used to express communal or individual historic experiences, and others were for contemplations. Like any poetic compositions, psalms have phonemic patterns with repetitions, for instance Ps. 67, where this pattern was repeated: "Let the peoples praise you, O God; let all the peoples praise you." The psalms are one hundred and fifty in number; though the numbers and verses are a recent development for easy reading.

The word psalm is derived from the Hebrew word tehillîm, or in Greek Ψαλμοί which means praises or songs of praise.[2] In ancient Israel, songs were used in worship. For instance, after the crossing of the Red Sea, Moses led the Israelites in songs of thanksgiving. Miriam also led the women in dancing and singing the refrain with tambourine (Ex 15:1- 21). Hannah also prayed in songs when God answered her prayer (1Sam 2:1-10). However, most of the psalms in the Hebrew Scriptures are attributed to David as the composer.

In the New Testament, Jesus quoted the psalms on several occasions. In Mt. 21:16, he outwitted the Pharisees with Ps. 8:2: "Out of

---

[2] Stewart McCullough, The Interpreter's Bible, Vol. IV, ed. George Buttrick et al (Nashville, NY: Abingdon Press, 1955), 3.

the mouths of infants and nursing babies you have prepared praise for yourself." When the Jews wanted to stone him to death, Jesus re-called Ps. 82:6 (Jn. 10:34: "Is it not written in your law, 'I said, you are gods'?). He quoted the psalm when he talked about his betrayal in Jn. 13:18: ("But it is to fulfill the scripture, 'The one who ate my bread has lifted his heel against me," Ps. 41:9). Jesus directed Pilate to Ps. 110:1 when Pilate asked if He is the Son of God (Mt. 26:64). Before the chief priests and the elders (Mt. 21:42; Lk. 20:17), Jesus referred himself as the Cornerstone rejected by the builders as written in Ps. 118:22-23. On the cross before he died (Mt. 27:46), Jesus quoted from Ps. 31:5, "Father, into your hands, I commend my spirit;" and Ps. 22:1 "My God, my God, why have you forsaken me?" (Mk. 15:34). Thus, from the beginning of Christianity, psalms became an im-portant part of the liturgy. However, the Church omitted some im-precatory psalms and some verses of some psalms from public wor-ship because they were "somewhat harsh in tone and because of the difficulties that were foreseen by the Church from their use in ver-nacular celebration."[3]

Imprecatory, cursing, or vengeance psalms are examples of la-ment psalms used to invoke evil upon an enemy or a group of ene-mies of the psalmist. Lament psalms include both sadness directed at God and complaints directed at God's enemies. Some of the psalms sound very negative and contain curses which are expressed by an individual or group who are in pain, struggling, or who are

---

[3] Pope Paul VI, Apostolic Constitution Promulgation, The Divine Of-fice. Christian Prayer: The Liturgy of the Hours, Sec 4, (Boston: Daughters of St. Paul Publication, 2003), 15.

pouring out their distress and agony to God. Brueggemann defines lament psalms as "the voices of those who find their circumstance dangerous and difficult, and they do not like it."[4] Lament psalms are cries to God for help for the weak, the oppressed, the sick, those unjustly treated, the needy, etc. The laments not only express the inner state of those praying, but also seek to change this state.

A lament can be personal or communal. After the covenant on Mt. Sinai, the Israelites developed a special relationship with God. They prayed the lament psalms and other prayers to express to God their conditions and real life experiences in all honesty and faith. They trusted that God would respond. That is why lament psalms are always followed with thanksgiving in anticipation of a positive response.

In ancient Israel, some sicknesses were considered a punishment from God because of sins; so were natural disasters, war, drought, famine, untimely death, etc. Rituals and lament prayers were therefore offered to God for healing and forgiveness of sins. When there was a community disaster, the entire nation including men, women, and children would go into mourning. This meant fasting from food and drink, applying dust to their bodies, and wearing sackcloth. These rituals were performed for penitential reasons to avert God's wrath on the people; for forgiveness of their sins and restoration of their land. Thus, they lamented to God: "Can dust praise you or hope for your faithfulness?" (Ps 115:17). They reminded God of his

---

[4] Walter Brueggemann, "Psalms and the Life of Faith: A Suggested Typology of Function," Journal for the Study of the Old Testament, no. 17 (Je 1980): 12.

covenant with their fathers; and provided him with reasons to hear their prayers.

Furthermore, Israel's lament psalms were for justice against corrupt people, enemies, sinners, sorcerers, etc., and they often saw themselves as innocent people who were being "persecuted without cause."[5] They prayed for revenge against their foes with these words, "Repay them according to their evil works" (Ps 28: 4); "Make their eyes darkened... and remove them from the book of life." (Ps 69: 23, 28). Sincere lament psalms were common among the Israelites because God was their only source of hope and he never let them down.

In our contemporary world, we still face the same atrocities, as the ancient Israelites, in the form of persecutions, corruption, injustice, false accusation, abuse of every kind, lynching, assassination, illness, pandemic, tribal conflicts, war, ethnic cleansing, genocide, terrorist attack, human trafficking, slavery, chaos, etc. The United States of America has recently experienced the marching for justice in unprecedented numbers after the killing of George Floyd. In cities across the country, thousands of people, from all races, are giving voice to the grief and anger that generations of African Americans have suffered at the hands of the system. Young and old, black, white, yellow, red, and brown have joined together to say: "Enough is enough!" Also with the recent outbreak of the Coronavirus disease which has ravaged the entire world, many people have wondered: Is God not capable of saving humanity? Is God punishing us for our

---

[5] Sigmund Mowinckel, The Psalms in Israel's Worship, (Grand Rapids, MI: William B. Eerdmans Publishing Company, 2004) 4.

sins? These questions and our helpless situation, evoke in us the desire to cry to God for help, like the Israelites.

The only difference however, is that we don't know how to cry to God with sincerity of heart. Sometimes we might be honest, but not "dialogical, sometimes we are politely dialogical but unable to be honest."[6] Sometimes we pretend or claim that all is well, instead of admitting that we don't have it all. What a false life! What we need is radical faith in God, a faith that can move mountains, and to present our needs honestly to God. St. Luke (11: 9) tells us to ask and we shall receive. We should therefore not hesitate to ask.

Psychologists admit that tears and lamenting (talking therapy) are very important therapy for the wounded soul. When pain is suppressed, it becomes as deadly as cancerous cells. St. Thomas Aquinas, similarly agrees that tears are a remedy for sorrow, and that pain hurts more when it is repressed.[7] Jesus himself used imprecatory statements when he noticed the hypocrisy of the Pharisees and the Scribes: "Woe to you Scribes and Pharisees, hypocrites!" (Mt. 28:13-39). In using such language, Jesus is not using the spirit of condemnation; but rather the attitude of: "You could do better than this." "Stop!" "Listen, believe, and be saved."

Another instance when Jesus used imprecatory psalm was before his death. Jesus cursed his betrayer: "The Son of man goes as it is written of him: but woe to that man by whom the Son of man is

---

[6] Walter Brueggemann, "From Hurt to Joy, from Death to Life." Interpretation 28, no. 1, (Jan. 1974): 5.

[7] St. Thomas Aquinas. The Summa Theologica of St. Thomas Aquinas, Vol. 1. (New York: Benziger Brothers, Inc., 1947) 754.

betrayed! It would have been better for that man if he had not been born" (Mt. 26:24). St. Paul likewise used imprecatory statement in his first letter to the Corinthians (16:22): "If anyone has no love for the Lord Jesus Christ, let him be accursed. Maranatha!" Furthermore he cursed anyone who would preach any gospel other than the one he preached and that which was received by the Galatians (1:8-9). These imprecatory statements are not a matter of personal revenge, but rather the zeal for God's justice and zero tolerance of wicked activities.

The Lament Psalms are still relevant today and that is why they were not removed entirely from the Bible. But the challenges are: Under what circumstances can they be prayed and what should be the intention of the one using imprecatory psalms? Does the indignation which burns so hot warrant the use of imprecation? Is it a righteous indignation and zeal for God's justice, or actually for personal revenge?

In 1970, the Apostolic Constitution of Pope Paul VI omitted from public worship Psalms 58, 83, 109, as well as nineteen other psalms from which one or two verses were omitted[8] because the curses in them are somewhat harsh in tone as explained above. Many scholars have frowned on this issue of removing some psalms from public worship as, "not being open to all God's word."[9] Martin

---

[8] William L. Holladay, The Psalms Through Three Thousand Years: Prayerbook of a Cloud of Witnesses (Minneapolis, MN: Augsburg Fortress Publishers, 1996), 304.

[9] Delores Dufner, "With What Language Will We Pray?" Worship 80 no. 2, (March 2009): 154.

Shannon agrees with Walter Brueggemann that the removal of the cursing psalms affects the integrity of the Psalter, thus breaking their train of thoughts and distorting the message of the psalms in their entirety.[10] Shannon continues that to deny the cries of vengeance is not only to deny the realities of evil, but also to deny God's rule over every aspect of human life. Also the removal of some psalms does not show authenticity of worship, as praying the cursing psalms reflects our honesty and true selves before God. Finally, Shannon concludes that the removal does not recognize the unity of the church; as the church is supposed to weep with those who are weeping.[11]

However, some scholars applaud the omission of some cursing psalms in public worship, and see it as "a wise decision, that even with explanation, the lines remain baffling and disturbing. How much more perplexing will they be to people uninitiated in Bible study?"[12] For Holladay, the cursing language seems particularly difficult when such cursing closes a psalm during the Liturgy of the Hours.[13] For instance, the speaker of Psalm 143:12 implores: "In your steadfast love, cut off my enemies and destroy my adversaries, for I am your servant." According to Holladay, this verse was omitted as it would be difficult to recite it with its language of self-righteousness and contempt for the enemy. The American Bishops also agree that

---

[10] Martin Shannon, "A Certain Psychological Difficulty or A Certain Spirituality Challenge: Use of the Integral Psalter in the Liturgy of the Hours." Worship 73, no. 4, (July 1999): 302.

[11] Ibid, 307.

[12] Carol Stuhlmueller, The Spirituality of the Psalms (Collegeville, MN: The Liturgical Press, 2002), 154.

[13] Holladay, The Psalms Through Three Thousand Years, 311.

"certain verses of the psalms have been judged to be inappropriate in a given culture or liturgical context."[14] The Church, the Body of Christ, guided by the Holy Spirit, chooses to omit some cursing psalms from the Holy Hours and the Mass to accommodate all cultures, since all peoples in the Catholic faith use the same prayer book. Their removal does not mean the cursing psalms were excluded from the scripture, or that the church is not being honest in worship, or that the church is "picking and choosing only the appealing and consoling God's word,"[15] rather the church is trying to be an accommodating and sensitive Mother.

As the saying goes, "Language is power." It reflects our thoughts and attitudes and shapes us. The words we use in prayers, especially public prayers, matter a lot. To curse an enemy with these words, "may your children be fatherless and your wife a widow" (Ps 109:9), would just be unbearable in public worship. According to the scripture, "the soul that sins shall die" (Ez 18:4), so why curse innocent people? Psalm 109 is a pure imprecatory psalm. Its desire for vengeance not only targets the enemy, but also his wife, children, ancestors, posterity and any future remembrance of his name. If such cursing psalms were to be allowed in public worship, it would contradict the commandment of love that Jesus preached. The new commandment: "love your enemies and pray for those who persecute you," (Mt 5:44) takes priority over the psalmist's word.

The fact remains that cursing psalms are emotional prayers that reflect the faith of the psalmist and they are not doctrinal instruction

---

[14] Dufner, 152.
[15] Ibid, 154.

for Christians to follow. Certainly God has never been known to rush right out and do whatever we ask him when we are angry, for God does not delight in the death of a sinner but rather for his/her conversion (Ezek. 33:11). Many of the lament psalms are prayers of revenge, e.g. "O God smash the teeth in their mouths" (Ps 58:7). "Let death take my enemies by surprise; let them go down alive to the grave" (Psalm 55:15). "May they be blotted out of the book of life and not be listed with the righteous" (Psalm 69:28). These prayers describe human reality of pain and suffering, but does "not suggest that we should imitate or encourage the attitudes described."[16]

Moreover, Jesus is our role model. While on the cross, he used the words of Ps. 22:1 in lamenting: "My God, My God, why have you forsaken me?" (Mt 27:46). Jesus never condemned those who crucified him, rather he asked God to forgive them. St. Stephen, the first martyr, also prayed for God to forgive those who stoned him to death (Acts 7:60). These examples demonstrate a change from the retributive justice of "an eye for an eye," to "love your enemies" (Mt 5:38-46). It was Mahatma Gandhi who says that "an eye for an eye leaves the whole world blind." Violence will never heal the world, love will. Thus, if we keep cursing those we deem cruel, then we are no better than the oppressors. Certainly, we can't solve violence with violence.

---

[16] Kathleen A. Farmer, "Psalms," in Women's Bible Commentary: Expanded Edition with Apocrypha, ed. Carol A. Newsom and Sharon H. Ringe, Original print, 1992 (Louisville, KY: Westminster John Knox Press, 1998), 149.

The attitude of revenge is explicitly illustrated in a story I received through a WhatsApp message. Though I am not sure of the source, it clearly shows the sad reality of revenge.

A British hostage released in 1990 from his kidnappers was asked if he wanted a revenge on his captors. He replied that he did not, for such attitudes are self-destructive and he did not wish to harm himself in that way. A fellow hostage was asked the same question, he responded that he could not get the experience out of his mind. He felt that his captors should be chained for forty years, the cumulative amount of time he and his fellow hostages were chained. A decade after their release these same two men got in contact with each other. Talking about their experience of torture, one asked the other: "Have you forgiven those who tortured us during the hostage?" The man admitted that he couldn't get even the tiniest bit of the experience out of his mind. He couldn't forgive them because every time he remembered what had happened, he was filled with bitterness, and dominated by the spirit of revenge. He was left with no outlet for his desire to retaliate. His friend replied: "In that case my friend, you are still a hostage and being tortured. However, not by our captors, but rather by yourself."

As human beings, there are times when our hearts are filled with sorrow and vengeance, and God's perceived silence needs to be broken. When things fall apart, e.g. loss of a job, death of a loved one, false accusation, injustice, natural calamities, murder of an innocent person, terrorist attacks, wars, ethnic cleansing, etc., these evoke feelings of rage and anguish in the victim. In the heat of these emotions, there is always the temptation to take matters into our own hands.

Brueggemann calls this process a movement from "orientation to disorientation, and to a new orientation."[17] When we move from the sense of security and joy (orientation) to circumstances that are not pleasant, but filled with agony and pain (disorientation), the solution is to cry out to God in faith, which may lead to transformation or new orientation. This transformation evokes strong faith and gratitude to God.

While we may lament as much as we want, we must leave vengeance to God, (Rm 2:6-8). Ultimately, God is not bound to act in human-guided ways. For this reason, the church sometimes uses lament psalms (not cursing psalms) during liturgies to be in solidarity with all her members who are suffering in different parts of the world, with the hope of rising with Jesus in the newness of life (Rm 6:4). It is during the liturgy that the entire praying community gathers to support one another, and the liturgy reminds us that no one stands alone in dealing with suffering.[18]

Jesus preached the language of love, so we do not pray for our enemy's path to be slippery, (Ps 35:6), but rather for him/her to turn to God and be saved (Mt 5:44). Christ encourages forgiveness of our enemies and praying for them, rather than violent expression of hatred for them (Mt. 5:43-44). It is only a sadist who takes delight in the misfortune of others. Although human nature reacts quickly to pain and agony, sometimes "doing nothing" as Jesus modeled when

---

[17] Walter Brueggemann, "Psalms and the Life of Faith: A Suggested Typology of Function," Journal for the Study of the Old Testament, no.17 (Je 1980), 6.

[18] Chinchar, Colloton, and O'Connor, 55.

he was scourged, brings order. In the same way, cursing someone cannot be justified theologically, in terms of altruistic concern for victims of injustice.[19]

Living in a chaotic world with its culture of hatred, ethnocentrism, racism, war, genocide, tribal conflicts, sexual, physical, and emotional abuse, terrorist attack, economic crises, murder, false accusation, injustice, natural disasters, political instability, corruption, etc., we ask ourselves: "Where is God in our distress"? In praying the Lament Psalms, we look to God who knows when to act. If God could take care of the birds and the lilies of the field (Lk 12:22ff), how much more will he take good care of our needs? Through the prayerful use of the lament psalms, we communicate our confidence, dependence and trust in the steadfast love of God as we celebrate Jesus' paschal mystery of dying and rising. Simultaneously, in using the lament psalms, we celebrate our daily dying and rising as we complete what was lacking in Jesus' suffering for the sake of His Body, the Church (Col. 1:24).

Finally, while using cursing psalms is understandable as we pour out our bitter experiences to God, we are to bear in mind that those harsh imprecations reveal human nature and the psalmist's emotions. They are not commands or instructions from God.

---

[19] James L. Crenshaw, The Psalms: An Introduction (Grand Rapids, MI: William B. Eerdmanns publishing Company, 2001), 68.

Chapter 3

FULFILLING A VOW MADE TO GOD

"If it is hard to give to whoever asks, it is still harder to let what belongs to us to be taken without asking it back. When Charity is deeply rooted in the soul, it shows itself exteriorly."
—St. Thérèse of Lisieux (*Story of a Soul*)

Psalm 66 (NABRE)

1 For the leader. A song; a psalm.
2 Shout joyfully to God, all the earth; sing of his glorious name; give him glorious praise.
3 Say to God: "How awesome your deeds! Before your great strength your enemies cringe.
4 All the earth falls in worship before you; they sing of you, sing of your name!"
                        Selah
5 Come and see the works of God, awesome in deeds before the children of Adam.
6 He changed the sea to dry land; through the river they passed on foot. There we rejoiced in him,
7 who rules by his might forever, His eyes are fixed upon the nations. Let no rebel rise to challenge!
                        Selah
8 Bless our God, you peoples; loudly sound his praise,
9 Who has kept us alive and not allowed our feet to slip.
10 You tested us, O God, tried us as silver tried by fire.

11 You led us into a snare; you bound us at the waist as captives.

12 You let captors set foot on our neck; we went through fire
   and water; then you led us out to freedom.

13 I will bring burnt offerings to your house; to you I will
   fulfill my vows,

14 Which my lips pronounced and my mouth spoke in my
   distress.

15 Burnt offerings of fatlings I will offer you and sacrificial
   smoke of rams; I will sacrifice oxen and goats.

Selah

16 Come and hear, all you who fear God, while I recount
   what has been done for me.

17 I called to him with my mouth; praise was upon my
   tongue.

18 Had I cherished evil in my heart, the Lord would not have
   heard.

19 But God did hear and listened to my voice in prayer.

20 Blessed be God, who did not reject my prayer and refuse
   his mercy.

Introduction

Praising God with the psalms is one of the rituals inherited from
the traditional Jewish people. As explained in chapter two, the Book
of Psalms contains hymns that were used by ancient Israelites in their
daily worship of God through praise, thanksgiving, lament; asking
for the forgiveness of sins, for protection, for favor, and healing. This
reflection is on Psalm 66, which is a thanksgiving psalm, probably
used in the temple to fulfill vows made to God in times of distress.

Vows are covenantal relationships between groups or individual, and in this case, God. It is taken seriously with thoughtfulness since the Scriptures encourage one to pay what one has vowed (Ex 30:1-2; Eccl 5:4). Vows are very important in the Hebrew world so much that women and young girls were not considered capable of making a standard vow without the permission of their husbands and fathers respectively (Ex 30:3-16).

In Psalm 66, the unidentified individual joyfully fulfills vows to God through an abundant sacrifice which his mouth proclaimed while in distress. What issues did the psalmist struggle with? What is the significance of emphasizing the need for "all the earth" to praise God on behalf of the answered prayers of the Israelites? Why were vows made in ancient Israel? Do unfulfilled vows affect an individual? This reflection will analyze these concerns as well as the theological and spiritual preoccupation of Psalm 66.

Exegesis

Psalm 66 was probably sung during a national festival[1] in post-exilic Israel when the remnant looked back and recounted what God had done for their forefathers. It was probably a post-exilic psalm because of the series of suffering imagery in verses 9-12; which depicted exilic slavery and humiliation. Later however, God led them to freedom. Psalm 66 could be a ritual dialogue between the temple

---

[1] Robert Davidson, The Vitality of Worship: A Commentary on the Book of Psalms (Grand Rapids, MI: William B. Eerdmans Publishers, 1998), 206.

personnel who calls the worshippers to sing joyfully of God's awe-some deeds (vs. 1-12). The people, represented by an individual, re-spond with abundant sacrifices (vs. 13-20).

John Eaton believes that the sacrifice which was offered by the nation as a whole, rather than individually, might signify the re-ded-ication of the worshipers.[2] Thus, the psalm unites the Israelite nation along with the whole world, the past and present deliverance, as well as the unidentified individual. It is interesting to note that this psalm is only used in the Church during the Easter season and it begins with the same line as Psalm 100 "Shout joyfully to God, all the earth."

Structurally, Psalm 66 has two distinct parts; one is communal worship of God's "awesome deeds," probably sung by the leader of the liturgy (vs. 1-12) using plural verb forms and plural personal pro-nouns. The second part of the psalm is an individual praise for de-liverance (vs. 13-20) beginning with the first person singular, "I will bring burnt offering...." Konrad Schaefer suggests that it is a "hybrid between what appears to be a community hymn and an individual thanksgiving."[3] Hans-Joachim Kraus thinks that these separate hymns were joined together either because an individual incorpo-rated his praise with the community hymn or that it is an editorial work.[4] Fredrick Gaiser explains that there is something intentional

---

[2] John Eaton, The Psalms: A Historical and Spiritual Commentary with an Introduction and New Translation (New York, NY: The Continuum International Publishers, 2005), 244.

[3] Konrad Schaefer, Psalms: Studies in Hebrew Narrative and Poetry, ed. David Cotter, et al (Collegeville, MN: The Liturgical Press, 2001), 160.

[4] Hans-Joachim Kraus, Psalms 60-150: A Commentary, trans. Hilton Oswald (Minneapolis, MN: Augsburg Fortress, 1989), 38.

about the structure of this psalm rather than poor editing because as the Israelites were called to praise God, one can either cringe (v. 3) or worship (v. 4).[5] There is an interplay of structure and vocabulary in the psalm and there are also parallel movements. Perhaps the community's thanksgiving evokes in the psalmist the urge to praise God and the willingness to testify to God's awesome works. Thus, what the Israelites represent to other nations is what this unidentified individual is to the Israelites.

Verses 1-7 have a series of imperatives to praise God, not only by the Israelites but also by "all the earth," "the peoples," and "the children of Adam." This inclusion might indicate that the redemption of Israel is the redemption of the whole earth,[6] and to signify that God is the God of all the nations since "his eyes are fixed upon the nations" (v. 7c). Verse 4 ended with a Selah, probably for the people to pause and recount the deeds of the Lord. Selah is a Hebrew word which calls for a break in the singing of the Psalm. These awesome deeds are mentioned in verse 6: the crossing of the Red Sea and the Jordan River as recorded in Exodus 14:1-15 and Josh. 3:11-4:24 respectively.

In verse 6, there is a switch in the language, from speaking of the Israelites as "they" to "we." James Limburg states that this change in language structure by the speaker brings the past story to the here and now as if the speaker and the worshippers witnessed the event.[7]

---

[5] Frederick Gaiser, "Come and See What God Has Done": The Psalms of Easter," Word and World 7, no. 2 (1987): 213.

[6] Eaton, 243.

[7] James Limburg, Psalms, ed. Patrick Miller and David Bartlett (Louisville, KY: Westminster John Knox Press, 2000), 218.

The leader not only invites the people to "come and see" these great deeds, he also brings the remembrance of this ancient deliverance to the present, i.e., "There we rejoiced in him." Thus, the people as a community witnessed to the saving work of God, which was still active in their individual lives (vs. 16-19). As the Israelite community witnessed God to the "nations," this individual (v. 16) testifies to God's greatness to the Israelite community.

Furthermore, John Kselman and Michael Barré explain that verse 6 is an example of merism, "whereby the whole history of salvation is suggested by the mention of the crossing of the Red Sea and the Jordan."[8] Moreover, it is a conviction that God who controlled the waters at creation, also worked in the history of the Israelites. Verse 7 ends with another Selah, perhaps a pause to allow the worshippers to contemplate on the action of God in their history.

Additionally, "the peoples" are summoned again to bless God in verses 8-12 for keeping the Israelites alive and bringing them to freedom. The language shifts in verses 10-12 from the imperative command "to bless and praise God" to active verbs with God as the subject: "You tested us, O God, tried us as silver tried by fire." God is seen as the one testing them through fire and allowing them to fall into a snare. They became bound as slaves. Finally, they were defeated by their conquerors who placed their feet on Israel's neck as a

---

[8] John Kselman and Michael Barré, "Psalms," in *The New Jerome Biblical Commentary*, ed. Raymond Brown, Joseph Fitzmyer, and Roland Murphy (Englewood Cliffs, NJ: Prentice Hall, 1990), 536.

sign of complete defeat just as David did to Goliath (I Sam. 17:51). While in this trial, the Israelites remained confident and steadfast.

These imageries depict slavery, humiliation after a defeat, as well as the imagery of a metal that is being refined through fire (v. 8-12). All these imageries point to the exilic experiences. The cleansing fire imagery was also recorded by the prophets (Is. 43:2-3; 48:10; Jer. 6:29; 9:7; Zec. 13:9; Mal 3:2-3) as they described the afflictions of the exiled Israelites. Going through "fire and water" in verse 12 is a form of merism and it indicates all kinds of trials. In the midst of all these trials of passing through fire and water, the people were confident that God went through the hardship with them and led them out to freedom (v. 12b). God kept them alive and did not allow their feet to slip (v. 9). Verse 12 concludes the first movement of the psalm which is the community hymn.

From verses 13-20, the language shifts from first person plural, "you led us out of freedom" (v. 12b) to first person singular "I will bring burnt offerings to your house" (v. 13). This psalm could be a song of confidence by the community, represented by an individual as he claims his innocence: "Had I cherished evil in my heart, the Lord would not have heard" (vs. 17-19). The individual's suffering has nothing to do with sin since God heard him because he "had not cherished evil in his heart." This is an honest, self-examination thanksgiving and a declaration of innocence. The distress, though still remembered, has become light since God's mercy and deliverance are experienced.

Finally, the psalmist identifies himself as the beneficiary of God's awesome deeds and steps out to pay his vows. The individual's closing thanksgiving echoes the same structure of verses 1-9. Frederick Gaiser puts it well that as the leader of the song calls the community to shout for joy to God for his awesome deeds (v. 2), the individual responds with affirmation by the offering of sacrifices: "I will."[9] His argument is that the "deliverance of one person is the deliverance of all; since in caring for one person, God demonstrates anew his compassion and his presence." The psalmist could be a priest since they are required to offer sacrifices on behalf of the people who brought the sacrifice into the temple.

Some scholars regard the sacrifice offered by this unidentified individual as substantial and on a great scale. Schaefer explains that no one has to offer that much in a thanksgiving ritual.[10] For Eaton, this sacrifice might have been offered by the whole nation or its leader rather than by an individual; and it is a wholly devoted offering rather than the usual offering that is shared by the worshippers.[11] Although the sacrifices mentioned are many, it could be a proper sacrifice for the fulfillment of the vows made by the individual or the worshipers as the case may be. God delivered them from distress; thus, they felt the need to fulfill their vows since their prayer had been answered.

But why was the vow made? What issues did the psalmist struggle with? Perhaps the psalmist was falsely accused of evil practices as Robert Davidson suggested;[12] or perhaps a slanderous accusation

---

[9] Gaiser, "I Will Tell You What God Has Done for Me" (Psalm 66:16): A Place of "Testimony" in Lutheran Worship?" 141.

[10] Schaefer, 161.

[11] Eaton, 244.

[12] Davidson, 208.

was levied on him as Hans-Joachim Kraus explained.[13] Apparently, there is an indication that the individual was in distress (v. 14) but there is no proof that he was falsely accused. When someone is falsely accused in the psalms, it would normally be made clearly apparent to the reader. For instance, Psalms 27:12 declares: "Do not give me up to the will of my adversaries, for false witnesses have risen against me, and they are breathing out violence." In another place the psalmist sings: "See how they conceive evil, and are pregnant with mischief, and bring forth lies" (7:14). Other instances are Psalms 12:2; 58:3; 59:12, etc; all these psalms point to the experiences of someone lamenting about false accusation.

However, the language of the individual in verse 14 was the voice of one in trouble, and while in this agony, he made a vow which he had come to the temple to fulfill because God had answered his prayers. The individual's distress could be sickness, childlessness (such as in the case of Hannah in 1 Sm. 1:10-11, 24-28), enemies' attack, threat of death, child-bearing anguish, etc. No matter what the problem was, it was now over and this individual stepped out to offer abundant sacrifices of rams, oxen, and goats. This sacrifice is a whole burnt offering where the animals are totally consumed at the altar, which is different from the prescription of votive offering found in Leviticus 7:16. This sacrifice is followed by a pause—Selah, probably to allow the worshippers to reflect on the meaning of the offering as well as to watch the rising smoke, a sign that God has accepted the offering.

---

[13] Kraus, 38.

Subsequently, the psalmist proclaims to the community what God has done; "Come and hear, all you who fear God, while I recount what has been done for me" (v. 16). He testifies to God's deliverance with his mouth, probably in the form of storytelling. This structure is parallel to verse 5; however, while verse 5 appeals to the sense of sight (come and see), verse 16 appeals to the sense of hearing. Nevertheless, both verses (5 and 16) are witnessing to what God has done for the community and for the individual respectively. On one hand, the community is calling the children of Adam to come and see what God has done for the Israelites. On the other hand, the individual is inviting and testifying to the Israelites, who fear God, to hear God's deliverance. Hence, the focus narrows from "the children of Adam" to "all you who fear God."

Ultimately, as the Israelites recount the awesome deeds of God in history, the omnipotent God still works in their midst. Thus, the community witnessed to the past event (vs. 6-7) and the individual witnessed to the present deliverance (vs. 17-19). Schaefer suggests that come and see or hear is an invitation for the worshippers to contemplate God's wonders,[14] and instead of cringing as the enemy would do (v. 2), they would rather worship God as faithful Israelites (vs. 4, 13). Finally, the individual blesses God for answered prayers.

Apparently, the invitation for "the peoples" to bless God in verse 8 was responded to by the psalmist in verse 20; "Blessed be God, who did not reject my prayer and refuse his mercy." This response is an evidence that God is worthy to be blessed because of answered prayers on behalf of the Israelites and the individual. Thus, the revelation

---

[14] Schaefer, 160.

of God-self to the Israelites is not only for the sake of the Israelites, but also for the entire nations.

For this reason, the psalmist is witnessing who God is and what he has done for the people of Israel, while the Israelites are witnessing who God is to other nations. This witness involves the exodus and the exile events which are historic moments in the lives of the Israelites. The memories of slavery in Egypt and in Babylon preserve the faith of the Israelites and warrant them to seek God's face when in distress. The psalmist sought after God's face while in distress and found it; his response was to joyfully bless God with abundant sacrifice.

The Theological and Spiritual Preoccupation of Psalm 66

Psalm 66 is an example of how theology was practiced in ancient Israel. The people interpret God's action in their present life through the lens of their historical experiences, especially the Exodus and the exile events. This oral theological information is an avenue through which their cultural memories are transmitted from one generation to another. This type of theology is found in many places in Hebrew Scripture. For instance, before the Israelites were delivered from slavery in Egypt, Moses reminded them to tell their children their story when they would be asked, "'What does this mean?' They shall answer, 'By strength of hand the Lord brought us out of Egypt, from the house of slavery'" (Ex. 13:14). The Ten Commandments began with the Exodus story (Ex. 20:2) and the book of Deuteronomy made references to this salvation story in many places (Dt. 6:12; 7:8; 8:14;

13:5). Joshua also challenged the people about which God to serve, whether it is God who brought them out of slavery or a foreign god. The people responded: "It is the Lord our God who brought us and our ancestors up from the land of Egypt, out of the house of slavery, and who did those great signs in our sight. He protected us along all the way that we went, and among all the peoples through whom we passed" (Josh. 24:17). The prophets also recounted the Exodus story to the people of their time especially when they were not keeping the covenant (Jer. 34:13; Mi. 6:3-4). All these references tie the past experiences to the present situation just as Psalm 66 reflected.

The worshippers in Psalm 66 are confident of God's deliverance in the history of the Israelites which they as well were experiencing in their own lives. They made sincere and abundant offerings to fulfill their vows not out of what they would gain, but rather in thanksgiving to God who answered their prayers. They went further and invited the "children of Adam" to share in their celebrations, "come and see," "come and hear." The significance of this witness is the possibility that it might provoke faith in the God of the Israelites to the pagan nations. The Israelites' spirituality is to lead other nations to the truth about God whose eyes are fixed, not solely on the Israelites, but also on other nations (v. 7; see also Rm. 2:19-24). The celebration is important because God has answered their prayer and thus, vows made to God need to be fulfilled.

As mentioned earlier, the conditions that led to this vow are not clear, but in ancient Israel, vows were made for several reasons. Jacob vowed to serve God if God kept him safe to return to his father's house (Gn. 28:20-22). Jephthah made a vow to sacrifice the first to come out to meet him on his return home, if God granted him victory during his war with the Ammonites (Jgs. 11:29-31). Hannah vowed to dedicate her child as a Nazarene if God would heal her barrenness (I Sm. 1:11, 28), etc. All these are instances when vows were made in ancient Israel.

The Israelites were also careful in making vows and in fulfilling them since there are consequences of unfulfilled vows. The book of Numbers cautions: "When a man (or a woman) makes a vow to the Lord, or swears an oath to bind himself by a pledge, he shall not break his word; he shall do according to all that proceeds out of his mouth" (Num 30:2).

Psalm 76:11 warns: "Make vows to the Lord your God, and perform them." The book of Ecclesiastes declares that it is better not to vow than that one should vow and not fulfill it (Eccl. 5:5). Vows are sacred words that when spoken, are binding. No wonder the psalmist, in this psalm, was delighted to offer exorbitant votive sacrifice, more than what the law required.

Basically, the consequences of unfulfilled vows in ancient Israel were death and/or a curse. For instance, after the Israelites had vowed to serve God, they also declared that "whoever fails to keep this vow was to be put to death" (2 Chr. 15:10-15). The prophet Malachi explained: "Cursed be the cheat who has a male in the flock and vows to give it, and yet sacrifices to the Lord what is blemished (Mal. 1:14).

Vows are made to God to show commitment and trust in appreciation of who God is and what He does for us. In a relationship with God, we are counseled to keep our promises to him. However, God is always faithful, (Deut. 7:9; 2 Tim. 2:13) even when we are unfaithful to the vows we have made to Him. Psalm 66 is therefore an attitude we could exhibit in our relationship with God and in making promises to Him.

Conclusion

Psalm 66 reflects the Israelites' method of theology by connecting their past experiences with present situations. In other words, the Israelites understand their present situation through their past salvation story. In reflecting on this psalm, we noticed that it moved from communal thanksgiving to individual praise. It is out of joy that the psalmist told their story and desired that all those who fear God should hear it. In fulfilling the vow made, the psalmist offered a whole burnt offering over and above what was prescribed for a votive offering. Because God did not reject the prayers of their ancestors in slavery and in exile, God will not reject the prayer made in faith. The omnipotent God who acted in history is still the God who is acting in the here and now. Hence, the psalmist can "make a joyful noise to the LORD with faith."

Chapter 4

MARY OF BETHANY:
A MODEL IN PATRIARCHAL SOCIETIES

"Love attracts love! Mine rushes forth unto Thee. To love You Jesus as You love me, I must borrow your very Love; only then can I find rest."

—St. Thérèse of Lisieux (*Story of a Soul*)

Jn. 12:1-8 (NRSV)

Six days before the Passover, Jesus came to Bethany, the home of Lazarus, whom he had raised from the dead. 2They gave a dinner for him. Martha served, and Lazarus was one of those at the table with him. 3Mary took a pound of costly perfume made of pure nard, anointed Jesus' feet, and wiped them with her hair. The house was filled with the fragrance of the perfume. 4But Judas Iscariot, one of his disciples (the one who was about to betray him), said, 5"Why was this perfume not sold for three hundred denarii and the money given to the poor?" 6(He said this not because he cared about the poor, but because he was a thief; he kept the common purse and used to steal what was put into it.) 7Jesus said, "Leave her alone. She bought it so that she might keep it for the day of my burial. 8You always have the poor with you, but you do not always have me."

Introduction

For many centuries, women have been dominated at the hands of patriarchal society and treated as inferior to men. In many cultures all over the world, women are treated as helpmates, maids, and as property to be acquired by men. Women are to be seen and not heard, their abode is in the kitchen, they do not have a right to the inheritance, and their main function is to procreate and nurture children. This reflection suggests that Mary's fearless model of discipleship in John's Gospel is a model of discipleship for women who live in domineering patriarchal society.

In this passage of the Gospel of John, Mary's attitude is quite intriguing and exceptional in a Jewish patriarchal society where women are expected only to be seen and not heard. Indeed, Mary's bravery can be a model for women. What can this intimate encounter between Jesus and Mary of Bethany teach women and men who uphold a patriarchal culture that dominates women?

The story about Jesus having been anointed was narrated by the four Gospels, but in different ways. The story probably goes this way in the early life of the Church before the Gospels were written: a certain woman anointed Jesus during his public ministry before he was crucified. Matthew and Mark have similar accounts of an anonymous woman who anointed Jesus on the head with the setting being the house of Simon the Leper in Bethany (Mk 14:3-9, Mt. 26:6-13). The significance of their accounts are that they point the reader to the death and burial of Jesus, since the anointing takes place two days before the Passover when Jesus would be crucified. The anointing of

Jesus in Matthew and in Mark is even more crucial since no one anointed his body either before burial or even on the day of his resurrection (Mt. 27:57-61; Mk. 15:42-16:1-8).

The similarity of this story in Matthew and in Mark is understandable since Mark is a source for Matthew. Similarly, one would expect Luke to have the same version of the story since he also has Mark as his source. But Luke's account is totally different. Luke records that a sinful woman anointed Jesus' feet in the house of Simon the Pharisee. This anointing takes place in the early stages of Jesus' ministry rather than toward the end of it (Lk. 7:36-50). Thus, it is an occasion to teach the crowd the need for hospitality, love, and forgiveness, as well as to know that Jesus has the power to forgive sins.

John's version of the story is also different. The similarities between Mark's and John's accounts include: Bethany as the setting, the anointing pointing to the burial of Jesus, as well as the words regarding the poor. The significance of John's account is that the woman, who anointed Jesus, was named as Mary, the sister of Martha and Lazarus.

Interpretation of Jn. 12:1-8

This story comes after Jesus had raised Lazarus from the dead. Some Jews planned to kill Jesus since many had believed in him on account of this sign (11:45-53). Consequently, Jesus no longer walked openly among the Jews (Jn. 11:54). John placed this incident six days before the Passover, while Matthew and Mark placed it two days before the Passover. The Passover seemed to be the best time to arrest Jesus, since as a devout Jew, he was expected to attend the feast as many Jews were already in Jerusalem for purification rituals before the Passover (11:55- 56). Sure enough, Jesus returned to the home of his friends in Bethany, which was two miles from Jerusalem (11:18).

Bethany was the setting and also described as the village of Mary, Martha, and their brother Lazarus. The dinner was probably at their home since all the siblings were present. In Luke's Gospel, Martha was presented as the owner of the house when the two siblings welcomed Jesus (Lk. 10:38); but in John's Gospel, it is unclear who owns the house. However, the Bethany siblings hosted Jesus in their home possibly because he restored honor to their household by raising Lazarus from death. The fact that the names of these siblings were mentioned, along with the amount of perfume involved, seems to indicate that they were from a wealthy and famous family within the Johannine community, and it was a sign of honor and prestige. They were also important to the identity of Jesus especially with the raising of Lazarus, who was addressed as a friend to both Jesus and the disciples (Jn. 11: 11).

Similarly, Mary and Martha were loved by Jesus (11:5). Bruce Malina and Richard Rohrbaugh think that Mary was the elder of the two, since Mary stayed at home with their visitors while Martha runs out to greet and welcome Jesus (Jn. 11:20).[1] The fact that Mary used the family's wealth extravagantly is also another indication that she might be the elder sister. On the other hand, Martha seems to be the spokesperson of the family, as well as the one who serves the guests

---

[1] Bruce Malina and Richard Rohrbaugh, Social-Science Commentary on the Gospel of John (Minneapolis, MN: Augsburg Press, 1998), 200.

just as any elder or younger sister would do. Apart from blood relationship, this sisterhood might also represent a shared commitment
to the mission of Christ.[2] St. Paul addressed his co-workers in the
missionary work as brothers and sisters (I Cor. 1:1, Rm. 16:1, 3, 17).

The prolepsis of Mary's action is mentioned in chapter 11:2,
"Mary was the one who anointed the Lord with perfume and wiped
his feet with her hair." By alerting the reader of this event before it
was narrated, the author presupposes that his audience knew the
story of the anointing, and that it is connected with the raising of
Lazarus from the dead. Sandra Schneiders thinks that the proleptic
recall in 11:2 alerts the reader to the prolepsis of the Paschal mystery
in chapters 11 and 12.[3] Schneiders explains that in these two chapters, Jesus is symbolically executed by the religious authorities in
11:47-53. He was symbolically buried in the anointing event by Mary
in 12:1-8, and he was symbolically glorified by his triumphant entry
into Jerusalem in 12:12-18. This last episode was attributed to the
raising of Lazarus, which presents Jesus' power and victory over
death because the crowd that witnessed the raising of Lazarus were
the same people glorifying Jesus (12:17-18).

In verse 2, Martha served the meal as she performed her diakonia
role, which was also recorded in Luke 10:38-42. Lazarus' presence at

---

[2] Adele Reinhartz, "Women in the Johannine Community: An Exercise
in Historical Imagination," in A Feminist Companion to John, Volume II,
eds. Amy-Jill Levine and Marianne Blickenstaff (New York, NY: Sheffield
Academic Press, 2003), 23.

[3] Sandra Schneiders, Written That You May Believe: Encountering Jesus in the Fourth Gospel, 2nd ed. (New York, NY: Herder and Herder,
2003), 172.

the table with Jesus reminds the reader of the previous story and is an affirmation that it is in Jesus that one truly finds life. Mary has the central role in the story and became a representative figure for the Johannine community. Her actions will have a theological meaning for the disciples since it will point to the desire of Jesus for them to serve one another; "So if I, your Lord and Teacher, has washed your feet, you also ought to wash one another's feet" (13:14-15). Thus, in John 12:1-8, Mary was no longer sitting at the Lord's feet listening as a disciple (Lk. 10:38-42), rather she was acting out her discipleship role by anointing and wiping the feet of Jesus.

Mary's action in verse 3 is certainly extravagant as the effect of the oil fills the entire house. Gail O'Day explains that the lavishness of Mary's love and action was apparently enough for all the people present in the room to participate in it.[4] O'Day observes that it was the second time scent is connected to this family; the odor of death is now replaced with a fragrance perfume emanating from Mary's love. The dramatic explanation of the way the fragrant perfume fills the room, might portray the abundant life which everyone will experience at resurrection, and the good news that would soon spread to the entire world.[5]

---

[4] Gail O'Day, "John," in Women's Bible Commentary, eds. Carol Newson and Sharon Ringe (Louisville, KY: Westminster John Knox Press, 1998), 387.

[5] Dominika A. Kurek-Chomycz, "The Fragrance of Her Perfume: The Significance of Sense Imagery in John's Account of the Anointing in Bethany," Novum Testamentum 52, (2010): 340.

The conflicting issue of this anointing is that it was customary for slaves to wash the feet of guests before meals.[6] Why did Mary anoint the feet of Jesus, an act reserved for slaves, and why was the act done during the meal? Mary probably was showing her humility and devotion, as well as recognizing Jesus as her patron. In John 11:32, Mary knelt at the feet of Jesus which signified patron-client relationship and addressed him as "Lord." Perhaps, the act was done during the meal so that Mary could express publicly her love for Jesus. With Christ reclining at the table for a meal, and Mary anointing his feet, some scholars see this gesture of Mary as erotic[7] which echoes the voice of a lover in the Song of Solomon: "While the king was on his couch, my nard gave forth its fragrance" (Sg. 1:12). Mary Rose D'Angelo explains that this Song of Solomon's reference has Messianic overtones of kingly anointing while also retaining and intensifying the erotic charge.[8]

Another conflicting issue is that it was considered scandalous for a woman to touch the feet of a man and immodest to let down her hair in public.[9] Mary's action of letting down her hair might have occurred privately since Jesus was not obviously dining in a public

---

[6] Samuel Ngewa, "John," in African Bible Commentary, ed. Tokunboh Adeyemo et. al (Nairobi, Kenya: WordAlive Publishers, 2006), 1277. See also, Malina and Rohrbaugh, 205.

[7] Mary Rose D'Angelo, "Mary 2," in Women in Scripture: A Dictionary of Named and Unnamed Women in the Hebrew Bible, The Apocryphal/Deuterocanonical Books and The New Testament, eds. Carol Meyers, Toni Craven, and Ross Kraemer (Grand Rapids, MI: Wm. B. Eerdmans Publishers, 2001), 120.

[8] D'Angelo, 120.

[9] Malina and Rohrbaugh, 205.

place; nonetheless, she was not ashamed to demonstrate her love for Jesus which seemed to contradict their cultural values.

Basically, Mary's anointing is symbolic and might represent her prophetic role[10] since in Israel prophets anointed the king, such as the anointing of Saul and David by Samuel (I Sam. 10:1-8; 16:1-13). Nevertheless, the anointing in ancient Israel was on the head as recorded in Matthew's and Mark's accounts. Some scholars think that John's author confused the stories in the synoptics because of the fact that Mary anointed Jesus' feet rather than head and wiped the oil with her hair.[11] Anointing on the head is a ritual that elevates one's status, such as that of priests, kings, and prophets, while anointing the whole body indicates preparing a dead body for burial (Jn. 19:39-42). But in this sacred text, neither the head nor the whole body was involved. Malina and Rohrbaugh believe that this anointing points to the forthcoming transformative action of Jesus—the washing of the disciples' feet. Similarly, it anticipates the death and burial of Jesus, as well as the love commandments of Jesus: "I give you a new commandment, love one another" (13:34-35). Thus, Mary became the first disciple to live out this commandment of love.

Ultimately, Mary's anointing has religious significance. Apart from being expensive, the oil is also from a perfume made from pure nard which points to the holiness of Jesus. Essentially, Mary's role in this passage points to her place in Johannine community. She is a disciple, a prophetic figure, as well as a friend of Jesus. As someone with religious authority, Mary blesses Jesus and becomes a model for

---

[10] Reinhartz, 23.

[11] Kurek-Chomycz, 348.

Him. Her anointing also introduces the acclamation of Jesus as the King of Israel which will take place during Jesus' triumphant entry into Jerusalem (12:12-15).

The challenging questions that beg for answers are: Did Mary anoint the feet of Jesus because He raised her brother from the dead? Was it because she thought Jesus was going to be the king of Israel? Did Mary have a premonition that Jesus was going to be killed, or was it only an expression of intimate love? Being a contemplative prophetess, it could be that she had an intuition of Jesus' imminent death and hence she preferred to honor Jesus while he was still alive. Jesus confirmed this realization, "Leave her alone. She bought it so that she might keep it for the day of my burial."

Granted, Mary's action points to the anointing of Jesus' body after crucifixion. However, her action is contrary to the action of Nicodemus who secretly anointed the body of Jesus before burial because he was afraid to profess faith in Jesus publicly (3:1-15; 7:50-52; 19:39). Both the attitudes of Mary and Nicodemus illustrate the contrasting models of discipleship, as well as the duality in John's Gospel: the contrast between light and darkness, belief and unbelief, day and night, etc. Nonetheless, Nicodemus completed what Mary had started, as he secretly but royally anointed Jesus' dead body. Mary's extravagant gesture reflects her good action which is worthy of remembering, and it corresponds to the closing words in Mark's and Matthew's accounts; "Wherever the good news is proclaimed in the whole world, what she has done will be told in remembrance of her" (Mk. 14:9; Mt. 26:13).

The gesture of Mary as a true disciple is contrary also to the attitude of Judas whom the narrator depicted as the one who would betray Jesus. It is interesting to note that wherever Judas' name is mentioned in John's gospel, the author would refer to his betrayal of Jesus,
which suggests the prior knowledge of Judas' action to the implied
audience (6:71; 13:2; 18:2, 5). Judas is a foil character in this story
because he did not desire any relationship with Jesus.[12] On the other
hand, Mary is a true disciple of Jesus who, unlike Judas, knows Jesus:
"Lord, if you had been here, my brother would not have died." Similarly, she believes in Jesus: "When Mary came where Jesus was and
saw him, she knelt at his feet" (11:32). There is mutual knowing and
loving between Jesus and Mary, contrary to the relationship Jesus
had with Judas, (11:5). Mary honors Jesus, but Judas, in the name of
loving the poor, ridicules Mary's gesture. The challenge-riposte is the
statement of Judas:[13] "Why was this perfume not sold for three hundred denarii and the money given to the poor?" But the narrator explains that Judas did not actually love the poor since he was after the
monetary value of the oil and primarily concerned with his own selfish gain.

Gail O'Day explains that Judas tries to establish a situation of "ei-
ther/ or" love: either one loves the poor or loves Jesus. On the other
hand, Mary demonstrates "both/and" love: one can love both Jesus
and the poor.[14] The challenge-riposte of Judas does not put Mary to

---

[12] Mary Margaret Pazdan, Becoming God's Beloved in the Company of
Friends: A Spirituality of the Fourth Gospel (Eugene, OR: Cascade Books,
2007), 54.

[13] Ibid.

[14] O'Day, 388.

shame since Jesus' timely response affirms the honor in her actions. The denouement is the statement of Jesus: "Leave her alone. She bought it so that she might keep it for the day of my burial. You always have the poor with you, but you do not always have me." With this statement, Jesus takes away the burden from Mary and makes it his own. This statement also might make a mockery of the concern of Jesus for the poor. Jesus is not ignoring the needs of the poor, rather he is rebuking the attitude of Judas who is actually defrauding them. At the same time, he was connecting the anointing with his death.

Application of the Pericope to a Patriarchal Culture

Patriarchal culture is a social organization marked by the supremacy of men; the inheritance of property and reckoning of descent are in the lineage of men. This notion ultimately creates an unequal relationship between men and women in the society. At times this patriarchal culture becomes very cruel and yet it is not recognized as oppressive by some in society, but rather seen as a way of life. Many women also accepted the superiority of men and thus when abuse occurs within the family they accept it as normal, and a sign of love. [15] Some reasons behind this kind of thinking are: wives are to be submissive to their husbands; men are physically stronger than women; women are created from the rib of Adam; men propose marriage and ask for the woman's hand in marriage; women take the husband's family name after marriage; in some cultures, men pay the

---

[15] Adaku Helen Ogbuji, Dealing Effectively with Domestic Abuse: The Ministry of Reconciliation and Healing (Nairobi, Kenya: CUEA Press, 2015), 30.

bride wealth or dowry during the marriage ceremony; and in most families men sustain the financial burden of the family.

The cultural domination of women come in many forms: sexual, physical, emotional, economic, religious, and social. Sexual domination is a form of marital rape, sexual harassment, incest, and sexual abuse. Physical supremacy takes the form of kicking, slapping, punching, hair-pulling, stabbing, choking, pushing, beating, and biting. Emotional control uses degrading words, negative criticism, social isolation, intimidation, name-calling, or harming a woman's self-worth in order to put her down; while economic power is denying the woman an inheritance right, as well as an opportunity to own property in her name, or to be gainfully employed in order to be economically independent. This economic abuse is a strategy some men utilize to keep a woman in check, so that she may remain in the house as a perpetual beggar. Religious dominance is when a woman is marginalized spiritually; for instance, when a married woman is forced to belong to the religion of her spouse, or when she is denied the right to practice her belief system.

All these strategies are used in a patriarchal society where men control and dictate to everyone in order to maintain the status quo. Some men will even quote the Biblical creation story that women were created from the ribs of men, and thus, should be submissive to them. Nevertheless, St. Paul admonished: "Be subject to one another out of reverence for Christ" (Eph. 5:21). In another place Paul says: "There is no longer male and female, for we are one in Christ" (Gal 3:28).

Ultimately, both male and female are created by God, and for God, as well as for each other resulting in mutual happiness. Consequently, both are equal and share a common humanity. In spite of their obvious equality, patriarchal power has subjugated women to a situation where they are seen as objects to satisfy the desires of men and to procreate children for posterity. Some men even perceive the exchange of gift— dowry—as a way of "purchasing" women; thus, they treat their wives as an object to be used.

This patriarchal domination was also experienced in the history of the Church, when a woman's sexuality was regarded as a serious obstacle to the path of salvation for a man, and a disease that required a cure.[16] Barbara Andolsen explains that during the Middle Ages, many women connected their rejected bodies with the Body of Christ in the Eucharist as a comforting expression of piety. Women rushed from church to church, within the same day, to receive Holy Communion and be united with the Body of Christ.[17]

After centuries of silence and marginalization, many women from different cultures and different parts of the world started to speak out and reclaim their places in society. The bravery of Mary of Bethany could be held up as a model of discipleship for women who are still facing patriarchal domination. Reflecting on Mary's actions is quite insightful. Without words, she speaks louder than the fearful disciples; she witnesses Jesus in a culture that suppresses women's

---

[16] Barbara Andolsen, "Whose Sexuality? Whose Tradition? Women, Experience, and Roman Catholic Sexual Ethics," in Feminist Ethics and the Catholic Moral Tradition, eds. Charles Curran, Margaret Farley, and Richard McCormick (New York, NY: Paulist Press, 1996), 210-211.

[17] Ibid., 214.

ability to raise their heads. As mentioned above, Mary's character as a disciple is quite different from the attitudes of fearful Nicodemus and Judas who ridiculed the honor and devotion that she gave to Christ. Thus, Mary's boldness as a disciple could be a model for women who live in a culture that suppresses women.

In my counselling and formation ministries, I have encountered several traumatic episodes of some women who faced cultural exploitation. Imagine the following trauma: a girl who watched as her parents favored the boys; a female child who was not included in her father's will, with all his wealth given to the male child; a woman who was not allowed to purchase a parcel of land without a man co-signing for her; a single woman who became an object of ridicule because she didn't get married; a widow who was treated inhumanly after the death of her husband while also blamed for his death; a woman who gave birth to only female children and became an object of ridicule because she did not give birth to a male child; a female child whose genital organs were mutilated and she could not effectively function sexually; and the list can go on. I realized that the bitterness of experiencing domination could only be healed when a woman forgives her past, and accepts that she is worthy enough to love and to be loved without self-blame.

Mary's bravery is a sign of self-acceptance and self-love, even in the face of intimidation and criticism. She was not affected by her patriarchal culture which suppressed women. She was a disciple as she sat at the feet of Jesus learning the skills of discipleship just as St. Paul was educated at the feet of Gamaliel (Lk. 10:39; Acts 22:3). Although Mary learned in silence like any good disciple, she was not silenced. She became a model, not only for the disciples, but also for Jesus.

Mary demonstrated her discipleship and faith by witnessing Jesus with her words and her actions: "Lord, if you had been here, my brother would not have died" (Jn. 11:32). Mary Margaret Pazdan puts it well when she said, "being a witness to others is a continuous activity within God's household which encourages listening, openness, and responding."[18] No wonder Mary did not listen to the scorn of Judas who pretended to love the poor, when it was actually pure selfishness. Rather she went ahead to give that which she had—self-love—by anointing the feet of Jesus.

Conclusion

The fact that one cannot give what one does not have, means that the best place for women to start, is by loving themselves. Even the commandment of love has a condition: "Love your neighbor as you love yourself " (Mt. 22:39). When one does not have self-love, one cannot love others. Women who are nursing the wounds of intimidation, rejection, abuse, and domination sometimes blame themselves for the oppression. Some of them experience low self-esteem and see themselves as not good enough. This intimate encounter between Jesus and Mary of Bethany could teach men (who oppress women) to refrain from domination, and show women (who suffer oppression) that Jesus loves them selflessly. Women should see their services in our culture as having theological meaning because it is in

---

[18] Pazdan, 62.

line with Jesus' command "Wash one another's feet." Likewise, men should recognize that a woman's love and service to humanity/family must not be taken for granted. A woman's dignity must be respected, valued, and appreciated in the Church and in society just as Jesus appreciated Mary's love.

Thus, the way forward is for women in patriarchal society to develop positive self-esteem through self-love as Mary did. It is time to sit up and look straight into the eyes of men without fear. It is also time to discard the attitude and belief that men are superior beings. The Church could also empower women by encouraging and making room for active and inclusive participation of women during liturgy.

This reflection explained the action of Mary of Bethany and how she can be a model for women who are living in a domineering patriarchal culture. Human beings, although created equal, have turned the world into a society where gender matters. Male supremacy is clearly felt and seen on a global scale, with the derogatory term "a man's world" being used often. It is unfortunate that the headship of men is misinterpreted: "Be subject to one another out of reverence for Christ" (Eph. 5:21). In some patriarchal societies, it is only women who are required to be subject to men. The call for liberation and women's empowerment grew from the awareness of the oppression and realization that everything in life has been arranged for the advantage of men. This empowerment process is ongoing and it's high time that women learn that life is what we make it, not what it is, especially in societies that still oppress them. Life is about seeing possibilities and potentials in being a woman, and then brightening the world with these opportunities. Mary, as a woman, made a difference in a domineering culture and she became a model for women to follow.

Chapter 5

FREEING A DAUGHTER OF ABRAHAM

"Love alone have I ever given to the good God; with love He will repay me."

—St. Thérèse of Lisieux (*Story of a Soul*)

Luke 13:10-17 (NRSV)

10 Now he was teaching in one of the synagogues on the Sabbath. 11And just then there appeared a woman with a spirit that had crippled her for eighteen years. She was bent over and was quite unable to stand up straight. 12When Jesus saw her, he called her over and said, 'Woman, you are set free from your ailment.' 13When he laid his hands on her, immediately she stood up straight and began praising God. 14But the leader of the synagogue, indignant because Jesus had cured on the Sabbath, kept saying to the crowd, 'There are six days on which work ought to be done; come on those days and be cured, and not on the Sabbath day.' 15But the Lord answered him and said, 'You hypocrites! Does not each of you on the Sabbath untie his ox or his donkey from the manger, and lead it away to give it water? 16And ought not this woman, a daughter of Abraham whom Satan bound for eighteen long years, be set free from this bondage on the Sabbath day?' 17When he said this, all his opponents were put to shame; and the entire crowd was rejoicing at all the wonderful things that he was doing.

Introduction

In Luke's Gospel, the mission of Jesus was summarized thus: Jesus was anointed by God "to bring good news to the poor, to proclaim release to the captives and recovery of sight to the blind, to let the oppressed go free, and to proclaim the year of the Lord's favor" (Lk. 4:18-19). From this point in his narration, Luke fills his gospel with stories which reflect Jesus' healing of the oppressed, the sick, the infirm, as well as forgiving sinners, and proclaiming the good news. For the evangelist, Jesus disregards Judaism's laws—especially regarding the Sabbath and ritual cleanliness in order to liberate the captives. The healing of the crippled woman is one of those acts of compassion that showed Jesus' mission being accomplished.

This healing story appears only in Luke which means that it is derived from his private source that is commonly referred to as "L" source. In his narration of Jesus' movement toward Jerusalem (13:22), Luke inserted this healing story between the report of a tragedy in Jerusalem (13:1-9) and the parables about the kingdom of God (13:18-21). In this first century society, where honor and shame dictate the activities and identity of a person, those without honor suffer much shame. Such was the fate of this nameless and crippled woman who was incapable of standing upright. For eighteen years she was without honor until she experienced the love and compassion of Jesus.

In this passage, Jesus' attitude is quite different. He initiates the healing without any request from the woman. What theological message is Luke communicating in this story? Why was the sickness attributed to satanic forces? Could there be any meaning attached to the eighteen years this woman had suffered? What is the significance of the woman being addressed as the "daughter of Abraham?" This reflection will examine these questions as well as the theological and spiritual concern of Luke in this story.

Interpretation of Luke 13:10-17

This story of healing is set in the synagogue on a Sabbath day. Before this healing we didn't know where Jesus was, but only that he was teaching (chapter 12) since some of those around had related to him the tragedy of what had happened in Jerusalem (13:1-5). Jesus uses the opportunity to teach them about repentance in order not to perish like those who had recently died, and he presents the need to bear fruit with the parable of the fig tree. The evangelist then inserted this healing story with his usual phrase "Now he was teaching...." Luke uses various opening phrases that introduce new episodes; for instance, "One day, while he was... (5:17), Once while... (5:1), One Sabbath, while..." (6:1) etc. Jon Nelson Bailey observes that Luke used this narrator's voice forty times in the Gospel to indicate the progression of his narration.[1]

Jesus is teaching on a Sabbath "as was his custom" (4:16). This is important to notice as evidence that Jesus observed the Sabbath practices. In many instances in Luke's gospel, the evangelist attempts

---

[1] Jon Nelson Bailey, "Looking for Luke's Fingerprints: Identifying Evidence of Redactional Activity in 'The Healing of the Paralytic,'" Restoration Quarterly 48, no. 3 (2006): 147.

to balance teaching with miracle stories, probably to show the importance of both for his community. The evidence of this method of Luke is found in Luke 4:31- 37; 5:17-26; 6:6-11. In all these passages, Jesus heals in the middle of his teaching. Fred Craddock notes that the teaching of Jesus in this passage that describes the crippled woman, is his last teaching in the synagogue as he journeyed toward Jerusalem (13:22).[2]

The story presents the woman as "just appearing." It is unclear whether she was among the audience listening to Jesus. However, every pious Jew is expected to be in the synagogue on the Sabbath.[3] Perhaps, the woman has simply come to worship like every other Jew without expecting any healing. She has suffered this sickness for eighteen years and there are various suggestions as to her illness. John Gillman thinks that the woman might be suffering from osteoporosis,[4] while Samuel Abogunrin suggests that her being "bent over" could be caused by spondylitis deformans, a disease that caused the bones of the spine to fuse together into a rigid mass.[5] On the other hand, Alan Culpepper explains that the illness could be attributed to the spirit of weakness.[6] The sickness might have been

---

[2] Fred Craddock, Luke: Interpretation: A Biblical Commentary for Teaching and Preaching (Louisville, KY: John Knox Press, 1990), 169.

[3] Ogbuji, 118.

[4] John Gillman, Luke: Stories of Joy and Salvation, ed. Mary Ann Getty-Sullivan (Hyde Park, NY: New City Press, 2002), 127.

[5] Samuel Abogunrin, "Luke," in The International Bible Commentary, ed. William Farmer et al. (Collegeville, MN: The Liturgical Press, 1998), 1412.

[6] Alan Culpepper, "The Gospel of Luke," in The New Interpreter's Bible Vol. IX, ed. Leander Keck et al. (Nashville, TN: Abingdon Press, 1995), 273.

caused by a spinal cord disease. Nevertheless in Israel, sicknesses were attributed either to sin or to the attack of an evil spirit (4:33; 6:18; 7:21; 8:2; 9:42). An instance where deformity was attributed to sin was seen by the question the disciples asked Jesus before his healing of the man born blind: "Rabbi who sinned, this man or his parents that he was born blind" (Jn. 9:1-4). Jesus himself associated the woman's bent back with the bondage of Satan in verse 16. Regardless of the cause, the nature of her healing was unique because Jesus initiated it on a Sabbath, as he had also done in healing the man with the withered hand, as well as the man afflicted with dropsy (6:6-11; 14:1-6).

Generally, these Sabbath healings took place in the presence of the leaders of the people. However, there was no indication that those cured had faith or had sought healing. Each ailing person simply appeared on the scene, except for the man with the withered hand who had been listening to Jesus teach. Finally, each of the healings incurred the opposition of the religious leaders. Normally, in Luke's narration of healing genres, faith is directly linked to healing; for instance, the healing of the Centurion's servant, the woman with the hemorrhage, the cleansing of the ten lepers, the raising of Jairus' daughter, etc. Apparently, this crippled woman did not ask or show faith. Her circumstances were different in other ways: she could not stand upright and join others in proper worship; her ill health was attributed to an evil spirit which rendered her unclean. As a result of these circumstances, she could be facing double marginalization and perhaps suffering from an even lower social status.[7]

Significant also is the mention of her length of illness. According to the narrator, the nameless woman has been crippled for eighteen years. This number corresponds with the eighteen people who had been killed by the tower in Siloam mentioned earlier in the same chapter (13:4). Heidi Torgerson explains that since these eighteen men died through no fault of their own, it suggests that the woman's sickness for eighteen years is also not her fault and thus should not be regarded as a punishment.[8] Barbara Reid notes that the number of years of her bondage points to the two periods of servitude in Israel: eighteen years of bondage to Moab (Judg. 3:14) and eighteen years of affliction from the Philistines and the Ammonites (Judg. 10:8).[9]

Eighteen years was a long time to suffer from the bondage of Satan. Thus when Jesus saw her condition, he called out to her saying: "Woman, you are set free from your ailment." Luke Timothy Johnson explains that Jesus used a passive perfect tense indicating God's role in the healing.[10] Jesus not only uses pronouncement in this healing,

---

[7] Heidi Torgerson, "The Healing of the Bent Woman: A Narrative Interpretation of Luke 13:10-17," Currents in Theology and Mission 32, no.3 (January 2005): 180.

[8] Torgerson, 179-180.

[9] Barbara Reid, "Sabbath, the Crown of Creation," in Earth, Wind, and Fire: Biblical and Theological Perspectives on Creation, ed. Carol Dempsey and Mary Margaret Pazdan (Collegeville, MN: Liturgical Press, 2004), 72.

[10] Luke Timothy Johnson, The Gospel of Luke, Sacra Pagina Series, Vol. 3, ed. Daniel Harrington (Collegeville, MN: The Liturgical Press, 1991), 212.

but he lays his hand upon her, a gesture conveying both healing and blessing which is common to Luke especially in the Acts of the Apostles (Acts 6:6; 8:17- 18; 9:12; 13:3). Laying on of hands is also an attribute of Jesus' healing: the healing of the crowd and the healing of the leper, (4:40; 5:13).

In verse 13, the touch of Jesus restores the health of the woman "immediately." The word "immediately" is a common way through which Luke describes the miracles of Jesus and their effects. Bailey notes that Luke uses this immediate restoration of the sick person ten times in his gospel and six times in Acts; while Matthew used it twice and Mark never used it.[11] In response to the healing received, the woman praises God to show the connection of Jesus' work with God's saving power. She most likely came to the synagogue to praise God, and then never ceased glorifying Him because she recognizes that the power within Jesus to restore her health is actually from God. Her response connects with the previous statement of Jesus: "you have been set free" and indicates God's role in the healing.

Verse 14 describes the reaction of the leader of the synagogue. Clearly revealing his indignant reaction to the crowd, the synagogue leader focuses on the issue of the violation of the Sabbath law by quoting from Exodus 20:9-10. Craddock argues that although the leader cites the Sabbath law to the people, it is an indirect attack on Jesus.[12] Johnson explains that the leader deserves to be called a hypocrite because he confronts the crowd rather than Jesus directly and

---

[11] Bailey, 155.
[12] Craddock, 170.

uses a ploy of deflected anger.[13] In response, Jesus takes the burden from both the crowd and the woman and speaks to the leader directly. He refocuses his challenge to the needs and the dignity of the human person. Using the challenge- riposte device, Luke presents the statement of the leader who uses the Torah (Ex. 20:9-10), certainly to try to win the crowd over and shame Jesus.[14] His statement challenged the honor of Jesus who was respected by the people as Rabbi and healer.

Torgerson illustrates the parallelism of the argument between Jesus and the leader and how Jesus challenged each of his points:

- (Leader) "Six days exist on which work ought to be done.
- (Jesus) "Hypocrites! Each one of you on the Sabbath, does he not loosen his ox or his donkey from the manger and, leading it away, give it drink?"
- (Leader) "Therefore come on those days and be healed..."
- (Jesus): And this woman, being a daughter of Abraham whom Satan bound for eighteen years, ought not she to be loosed from this bond..."
- (Leader) "and not on the day of the Sabbath."
- (Jesus) "on the day of the Sabbath?"[15]

---

[13] Johnson, 212.
[14] Gillman, 127.
[15] Torgerson, 184.

In a culture that is centered on the core values of honor and shame, if Jesus' response was not convincing, he would have been ashamed. However, the challenge of the religious leader does not shame the crowd or Jesus because His argument is sound. Jesus makes an argument from the lesser to the greater, (argumentum ad maius), i.e., comparing the ox and donkey with the woman.[16] That is to say, if a donkey or an ox that is bound for a few hours can be loosed on a Sabbath, how much more this daughter of Abraham who was bound for eighteen years. The denouement of the challenge is the argument of Jesus which appeals to human experiences. Jesus argues that the woman is more valuable than animals, and the brief moment the animals had to wait to be watered is insignificant compared to the years this woman had to wait to be healed. Johnson argues that Sabbath is a time of liberation in connection with the redemption of debts and freeing of the slaves; thus, it is in line with the mission of Jesus to bring forth the reign of God to those who are bound by Satan.[17]

The argument of Jesus is that just as the people untie their animals on Sabbath in order to lead them to water, Jesus is also setting free and giving life to a daughter of Abraham who has been under the bondage of Satan for eighteen years. Hence, the healing of this woman celebrates the true meaning of Sabbath as a day of mercy, compassion, and liberation.

During the healing, Jesus addresses this woman as "a daughter of Abraham." This honor places the woman back to the covenantal

---

[16] Ogbuji, 119.

[17] Torgerson, 184.

community and within the reign of God. Her honor and dignity are restored because the claim of Abraham as an ancestor is the pride of every Jew.[18] This pride was evidenced in the admonition of John the Baptizer to the people who came for baptism: "Bear fruits worthy of repentance. Do not begin to say to yourselves, 'We have Abraham as our ancestor;' for I tell you, God is able to raise up children from these stones for Abraham" (Lk. 3:8). It is most likely that this unclean woman had been living outside the community of the covenant people because of her illness and was perhaps scorned by her neighbors. Jesus becomes her advocate and elevates her to the covenant community that he heads. He confers on her a status of dignity. This status of honor was also conferred to another outcast, Zacchaeus (a tax collector) when Jesus said: Today salvation has come to this house, because he too is a son of Abraham (Lk. 19:9). On the contrary, no name is given to the leader of the synagogue apart from clearly being included with the hypocrites. The honor of the healed woman is certainly a reversal of status which is Luke's favorite way of showing how Jesus lifts the lowly and brings down the powerful.

Verse 17 explains the reaction of the divided audience; while his opponents are put to shame, the crowd rejoices at the wonderful work of Jesus. Worthy of noting is the transition from "a leader" to "his opponents." It could be that this leader was the spokesperson of his group and thus was legitimately representing them before the crowd. The religious leader, who claimed to know the law and paraded in religious pride, was not only challenged, but also was shamed. Luke consistently portrays the religious leaders of the Jews

---

[18] Ogbuji, 120.

as the chief adversaries of Jesus, especially on the issues of what is lawful on the Sabbath, on the power of Jesus to forgive sins, on the violation of Jewish traditions, and on the association of Jesus with tax collectors and sinners.

On the other hand, Jesus was honored by the choric response and rejoicing of the people. The rejoicing and praising of God after every healing is characteristic of Luke. This summary statement of praise shows the response of those who witnessed the healing and how they received the healing.

Theological message and spiritual preoccupation of Luke

Luke's message is that the situation of the woman was not natural. Luke stresses the condition of the woman thus: "She was bent over and was quite unable to stand up straight." Anyone who is bent over will not be able to stand upright. By stressing her condition, Luke communicates that the woman was not the way she was meant to be. She needs to be liberated. Jesus' compassion initiates the healing. Words are not enough, so Jesus touches her. Luke is communicating that the touch of Jesus is a significant gesture to show how Jesus values every person, especially the oppressed in the society, and to show how he intends to bring about the reign of God. Jesus does not stop as the woman regains her health, but he also recognizes her dignity as the daughter of Abraham who deserves to reclaim her place in the community of the covenant people.

Jesus, in contrast to the religious leader, highlights the importance of compassion over legalism. He serves the needs of the

sick, the oppressed, and the poor at any time, without any law re-
strictions. This attitude of Jesus shows that the law should serve the
needs of the people, protect them, but not oppress them. For Jesus, it
is better to save a life and do good on a Sabbath rather than destroy
life or do harm (Lk. 6:9). Thus, Luke stresses the connection between
Sabbath, liberation, and freedom. He fills the gospel with stories to
convey this message: the healing of the man with a withered hand,
the plucking of the grain by the disciples, the healing of the man with
dropsy, as well as this healing of the woman who is bent over (6:6-
11; 6:1-5; 14:1-6; 13:10-17). Perhaps, there is a struggle within the
Lucan community on how to treat the Sabbath day. As a result, Luke
tries to explain that the Sabbath law and its observance should be
guided by compassion and liberating works following the examples
of Jesus.

Another theological implication of Jesus working on a Sabbath is
to reveal his Divine affiliation with God. For the Jews, God is the only
one who could work on a Sabbath.[19] God created the day of rest for
humanity, blessed it, and commanded that it be kept holy (Gen 2:2-
3, Ex. 20:8-11). Because Jesus works on the Sabbath, he makes himself equal to God (Jn. 5:18). On making himself identical to God,
Jesus emphatically states: "My Father is still working, and I also am
working" (Jn. 5:17). In another place, Jesus reveals himself as the
Lord of the Sabbath (Lk. 6:5) and this ultimately discloses him as
God.

---

[19] Mark Kinzer, Post-Missionary Messianic Judaism: Redefining Christian Engagement with the Jewish People (Grand Rapids, MI: Brazos Press,
2005), 91.

Furthermore, the issue of raising the poor from their condition and bringing down the rich is an important theme in Luke's gospel. This section of the scripture is one example that shows how honorable the poor are treated in Luke, in contrast to the way Jesus treated religious leaders who thought themselves superior and powerful. The religious leaders probably had expected Jesus to identify with them, support their view of law, as well as recognize their religious authority. On the contrary, Jesus identified mostly with the poor. Throughout the gospel, the Evangelist demonstrates this theme of honoring the poor and dishonoring the powerful. Examples: Mary's song of praise expresses God's mercy on the lowly while the powerful are brought low (2:51-53); Luke's beatitudes differ from those in Matthew because Luke contrasts the blessings of the poor with the woes of the rich (6:20-26); Luke calls the widow's mite "the greatest gift," and shuns the rich who were giving money out of their abundance (21:1-4). Also in the story of the Good Samaritan, Luke rejects how religious leaders value their profession rather than human dignity (10:25-37). Later in the parable of the great dinner where the host is disappointed with those initially invited to the dinner, Luke clearly explains how God extends his kingdom to the poor and infirm on the streets, roads, and lanes (14:15-24).

For the powerful and religious authorities, the utmost embarrassment was when Jesus dined with the Pharisees. Luke portrays Jesus not only as an ungrateful guest, but also that He condemns the Pharisees: he calls them fools and hypocrites, and says they ate with unclean hearts. Later, Jesus advises the disciples to beware of the hypocrisy of the Pharisees (11:37-12:1-4). In view of all these negative remarks, it is not surprising to hear that the Pharisees are very hostile to Jesus (11:53).

It is most likely that the struggle between Jesus and the religious leaders is a reflection of the conflicts between the Lucan community and religious leaders of that time. This community might be facing hostility on account of the Sabbath observance and having faith in Jesus. Perhaps Luke is demonstrating to his community the kind of life expected of them: a genuine Christian life that challenges oppressive authorities and favors the marginalized.

Conclusion

This healing story of the woman who was bent over presents her as a nonentity prior to her encounter with Jesus. Her significance manifested after the healing and she was reintegrated into the covenantal community, as well as honored with the highest dignity in Israel—recognition as a daughter of Abraham. A connection is suggested between the eighteen years she suffered with the eighteen people who were killed by the tower in Siloam earlier in the same chapter. The spiritual concern of the Evangelist, especially in the areas of interpreting the true meaning of Sabbath as a liberation day, is made very clear from this Biblical passage. Luke's story also reveals the respect Jesus has for human dignity and his option for the poor and the marginalized. This liberation theology of elevating the poor while bringing down the powerful no doubt has profound insights for Luke's audience.

Chapter 6

THE BASIS OF COURAGE IN THE MIDST OF LITTLE FAITH

"Just as a torrent sweeps along with it whatsoever it encounters on its course, even so, my Jesus, does the soul which plunges into the boundless ocean of Your Love draw all her treasures."

—St. Thérèse of Lisieux (*Story of a Soul*)

Mt. 14:22-33 (NRSV)

22 Immediately he made the disciples get into the boat and go on ahead to the other side, while he dismissed the crowds. 23And after he had dismissed the crowds, he went up the mountain by himself to pray. When evening came, he was there alone, 24but by this time the boat, battered by the waves, was far from the land, for the wind was against them. 25And early in the morning he came walking towards them on the lake. 26But when the disciples saw him walking on the lake, they were terrified, saying, 'It is a ghost!' And they cried out in fear. 27But immediately Jesus spoke to them and said, 'Take heart, it is I; do not be afraid.'

28 Peter answered him, 'Lord, if it is you, command me to come to you on the water.' 29He said, 'Come.' So Peter got out of the boat, started walking on the water, and came towards Jesus. 30But when he noticed the strong wind, he became frightened, and beginning to sink, he cried out, 'Lord, save me!' 31Jesus immediately reached out his hand and caught him, saying to him, 'You of little faith, why did you

doubt?' 32When they got into the boat, the wind ceased. 33And those in the boat worshipped him, saying, 'Truly you are the Son of God.'

Introduction

"Do not be afraid," Jesus says to Peter. How should we hear these words when we are in the midst of a worldwide pandemic that is ravaging life as we know it? How do we not panic when millions are being infected by the virus? We have witnessed the empty churches. Social distancing has become the norm, and thus home-based liturgies have been happening for many months. Across the globe, wearing a face mask is mandatory and regular washing of hands is encouraged. Despite being inundated with fear and anxiety of this Coronavirus pandemic, we saw courageous health care providers and first responders working tirelessly to attend to those infected with the virus, even when their colleagues and patients were dying. We have witnessed rampant hunger, and the benevolent souls who have reached out to feed those in need. We hear this slogan daily: "Stay home! Save lives! Help slow the spread of COVID-19!" We face financial difficulties because of the lockdown and the stay-at-home order. Millions of people became unemployed and have lost businesses. Many deaths have been recorded throughout the world. No place is safe. No one is immune to Coronavirus. The anxiety is so enormous that people were afraid and worried to leave their houses.

Apart from the Coronavirus pandemic that crippled the world last year 2020 and continues this year, there are also other disasters that fill people with doubt and fear. For instance, the 2020 tropical storm Laura and Delta that rendered many people homeless around Texas-Louisiana borders, the wildfire that has wiped out many cities, killed many people, and rendered many homeless in California, Oregon, and Washington States in the United States, as well as the 2019 wildfire in Australia that also killed many people. Other instances include: the Cyclone Idai that killed many people and rendered many homeless in May 2019 in Mozambique and other parts of South Africa. Hurricane Maria in September 2017 devastated the entirety of Puerto Rico, flattening neighborhoods, killing many people, and crippling the island's power grid. In 2011, the people living around the Caribbean and the East Coast of the U.S. experienced a bad storm called Irene that caused widespread destruction and killed many. On January 12th 2010, Haiti experienced an earthquake that killed between 46,000 and 316,000 people. In 2008, there was another terrible hurricane called Ike which devastated the people living in the Gulf Coast of Texas. There was hurricane Katrina in August 2005 that killed many people and rendered many homeless. And of course, the Galveston Hurricane of 1900 which remains the deadliest natural disaster in the history of the United States, killing over 6000 people including ten of our CCVI Sisters, and ninety orphans. These terrible storms washed away houses, overturned cars, killed countless people, and shattered the lives of many.

The apostles in this passage were emotionally devastated; they were caught in the storm while Jesus was absent. In our personal life storms, it can be easy to feel the absence of Jesus. Although the promise of Jesus is sure, "I am with you always to the end of age" (Mt.

28:20), there are times and circumstances in our lives when we doubt as did Peter and the disciples.

When as believers we are caught up in the storms of life, we question why there is tremendous suffering despite the existence of a loving God. Why do bad things happen? Actually, the question should not be "why" but "when will it happen?" This is because we live in a world where there are two forces—forces of good against evil, and two wills—the freedom and the willpower to choose evil rather than good and vice versa.

The pericope above was probably told to Matthean community who may have experienced or heard about Jesus' healings, miracles, and preaching. This Jesus was dead, but God raised him up, and now he has ascended into heaven. Possibly, the concern of this community could be: How can we survive without the physical presence of Jesus?

Reflection on Matthew 14:22-33

This story comes after Jesus had received news of the death of John the Baptist. Jesus withdraws in a boat to a deserted place by himself, either to pray or to reflect on what had happened to his cousin. Jesus is clearly aware that death awaits him as well. But the crowd would not allow him be alone, and they followed him on foot. Mark mentions that Jesus went with his disciples in the boat (Mk. 6:30-32), while in Matthew, Jesus went alone (Mt. 14:13). It is possible that the disciples either went on the boat with him, or that they walked on foot with the crowd, since the apostles would soon provide the five loaves and the two fish used to feed the multitudes. Jesus had compassion on the crowd, healed their sicknesses, and fed them. By feeding the crowd and dismissing them after he had healed and cared for them signifies that he was their Patron. Basically, as the head of their oikos (household), Jesus provides for the needs of his people, spiritually and physically.

The characters in the Matthean story of the storm are Jesus and the disciples. With Peter playing a major role as the spokes-person for the disciples. Apparently, the story has an ecclesial dimension. Benedict Viviano perceives the passage as a parable of the Church besieged with storm and sent out vulnerable into the unknown.[1] The Evangelist starts his story with Jesus making the disciples enter the boat. The phrase, "Jesus made them" indicates that it was a command. They had likey not wanted to enter the boat and leave Jesus behind. They may also have the need for prayer. Jesus, who had compassion on the crowd a few hours before this incident, is now sending the disciples away alone in order to pray. Eugene Boring notes that in redacting the Marcan version, Matthew emphasizes the separation of Jesus and the disciples: Jesus is "alone by himself " and the disciples are "far from the land" by themselves.[2] He concludes that the aloneness of the disciples and the storm story symbolize the suffering

---

[1] Benedict Viviano, "The Gospel According to Matthew," in The New Jerome Biblical Commentary, eds. Raymond Brown, Joseph Fitzmyer, and Roland Murphy (Englewood Cliffs, NJ: Prentice Hall, 1990), 658.

[2] Eugene Boring, "The Gospel of Matthew: Introduction, Commentary, and Reflections," in The New Interpreter's Bible, Vol VIII, eds. Leander Keck et al., (Nashville, TN: Abingdon Press, 1995), 327.

that the Church will experience in her mission. The storm also represents the anguish that the people of God face in their daily lives.

The setting of the story is in the middle of the sea. Mark places the destination of the disciples as Bethsaida (Mk. 16:45). On the other hand, Matthew omits the Marcan destination and explains that the disciples ended up in Gennesaret (Mt. 14:34) which is in the Northwest below Capernaum.[3] Boring clarifies that the feeding event could have taken place on the east bank of the Sea of Galilee, while the disciples got into the boat heading towards the west bank since they were crossing to the other side.[4]

The other setting presents Jesus alone praying on the mountain. The news of the death of John the Baptist probably disturbed him so that he needed to be alone in prayer with his Father. Apart from the introduction about prayer in 6:5-15, Boring notes that it was the first time in the gospel of Matthew that Jesus was said to pray. It always humbles me whenever I read of Jesus spending time in prayer. His solitude in prayer is a model for all Christians especially during the storms of life. As Jesus was praying, the disciples were alone in the middle of the sea battling with the strong wind. To be on the sea could represent the anxieties, dark powers, persecutions, and the images of death that threaten the goodness of life. However, in the middle of the disciple's distress, Jesus, who mediates the presence of God, is not with them.

---

[3] Daniel Harrington, The Gospel of Matthew, Sacra Pagina, Vol. 1 (Collegeville, MN: The Liturgical Press, 1991), 224.

[4] Boring, 327.

The incident takes place at evening, through the night to early morning. Harrington demonstrates that the time was around the fourth watch and the last watch of the night which occurred between 3:00 and 6:00 a.m.[5] This indicates that the disciples struggled alone without Jesus from evening to the early hours of the following morning. However, it could be that Jesus was with them spiritually, since he was most likely praying for them too. This notion is evidenced in the Marcan version who emphatically states that Jesus saw their agony (Mk.6:48).

After a stormy night of terror, Jesus comes walking on the water. This frightens the disciples even more because they thought that he was a ghost. This gesture is the conflict of this story, because Jesus who is both their Patron and sometimes their Broker before God, is doing what God alone does. In biblical traditions, only God walks on the sea (Job 9:8; 38:16; Ps. 77:19; Is. 43:16; 51:9-10; Sir. 24:5-6). For Jesus to walk on the sea reveals his identity as Divine. Matthew communicates the identity of Jesus by his power over the cosmos and by the use of the divine name: "It is I." Viviano elucidates that Jesus speaks with God's voice, "I am" and shares in the divine power to save.[6] Nothing could have given the disciples courage apart from the words of Jesus: "Take courage; it is I, do not be afraid." However, this divine name and encouraging words seem not to make any difference to the disciples. They wanted proof. The disciples still do not get it! Peter himself does not get it! As the representative of the strength and weakness of the disciples, Peter will challenge his Patron.

---

[5] Harrington, 224.

[6] Viviano, 658.

Prior to Peter's challenge, Matthew has been following Mark as his source, even though Matthew omitted the important phrase: "Jesus wanted to pass them by" (Mk. 6:48). Verses 28-31 are from a uniquely Matthean source since Mark ended with Jesus' entering the boat and to the disciples' amazement, the storm ceased, but they lacked understanding and experienced hardness of hearts. The remaining part of the Matthean story gives prominence to Peter as in his other stories; such as, the great confession of faith in Jesus by Peter at Caesarea Philippi and later the question of payment of the Temple tax (Mt. 16:17-19; 17:24-27).

To the amazement of the disciples, Peter challenges Jesus: "Lord, if it is you...." Although Peter uses the right Christological title that signifies his faith as a believer in the "Lord," his challenge could be compared to the confrontation of Satan in the temptation story, "If you are the Son of God" (Mt. 4:3, 6). What can we make of Peter's request to walk on the sea like Jesus? Was Peter trying to test Jesus' identity or did he desire to walk with his Lord? Peter wants proof of the divine presence of Jesus, and he desires to be empowered to walk on water. Jesus responded and redeemed his honor with the Divine name, "I am, come."

Peter gets out of the boat and walks on the water. Boring is of the opinion that Peter's problem is not only getting out of the boat (the community of the faithful), but that he also takes his attention off Jesus and focuses on the wind.[7] Peter's little faith could go so far, but it sometimes seems as if he makes progress of one step forward, and then falls two steps back because of his little faith. He does what

---

[7] Boring, 328.

every one of us does since our faith is neither absent nor perfect. It is little! And this "little faith" is a common phrase in Matthew's Gospel (6:30-33; 8:26; 16:8; 17:20). Peter looked away from Jesus because he was afraid of the strong wind and he began to sink.

Ultimately, Peter knows that Jesus is his only Savior and Patron. Thus, he cried out, "Lord, save me." Boring thinks that the cry of Peter is perhaps a community prayer adapted from the Psalms and the early Christian worship. The denouement of the challenge and the conflict is that Jesus reaches out his hand and saves Peter. In rescuing Peter, Jesus does what the Scriptures attribute to God. Psalm 144:7 explains: "O Lord, stretch out your hand and rescue me, deliver me from the mighty waters…" (Ps. 18:16; Jonah 2:1-10). Apart from Jesus restoring his honor through saving Peter, the Divinity of Jesus is also manifested with the strong wind ceasing at the presence of Jesus in the boat. Jesus is honored by the choric response of the disciples.

Matthew redacts the Marcan ending of this Biblical text since in Mark the disciples lacked understanding. They experienced hardness of heart even in their astonishment. On the other hand, in Matthew's account, the disciples are more positive. They bow down and worship Jesus saying, "Truly, you are the Son of God." Their confession counters Peter's initial challenge, which had echoed the voice of Satan during the temptation of Jesus. It is also the same confession that the centurion made at the foot of the cross in acknowledgement of Jesus' true identity as God's Son (Mt. 27:54). Harrington suggests that this response would become the disciples' post-Easter understanding of the identity of Jesus.[8]

---

[8] Harrington, 227.

The Evangelist tells this story to a community contemplating survival without the presence of Jesus. This community is mostly Jewish Christians who are persecuted and separated from the synagogue. Matthew's redaction might be a consolation to the Sitz im Leben of those struggling with the identity of Jesus. To illustrate the belief that Jesus is the expected Messiah and the Son of David, the Evangelist used many healing stories, cosmic stories, as well as teachings: for instance the healing of the Canaanite woman's daughter, the healing of the two blind men, the genealogy, the triumphant entry into Jerusalem, the argument with the Pharisees over whose son the Messiah is (15:17-27; 9:27; 1:1; 20:30-31; 21:9; 22:42), as well as this story. Matthew does not stop in demonstrating that Jesus is the Son of God and the Messiah. The Evangelist also establishes the fact that Jesus' presence in his community, and in the Church, is everlasting even during persecution: "I am with you always to the end of age" (28:20).

The confidence that Jesus is always with the Church or with the people of God is sometimes overcome by fear, doubts, and discouragement because of persecutions, sufferings, and trauma. But Jesus tells us, "Take courage, it is I; do not be afraid." How can we not be afraid when there is so much to fear? In fear, the disciples called Jesus a ghost. In fear, Peter courageously steps out of the boat, but his courage does not last long since his fear is manifested in his distracted attention to the winds. Joanna Adams, in explaining Peter's fear, compares it to the illustration of a teenager who is teaching her older father how to dance: "You'll never learn to dance if you are always thinking about how you look on the dance floor."[9] In the same way, no one will ever learn to live life to the fullest if all the attention is focused on the storms of life.

Peter is our model of strength and weakness. In the first place, it takes courage, grace, and faith to get out of the boat, as well as to focus on Jesus. Getting out of the boat in this case is to accept and acknowledge the reality of pain; to be gentle and patient with ourselves because healing takes time; to be open and remain vulnerable with the understanding that we are not God; to accept what we cannot change; to open ourselves to people that are a comfort to us; and to trust that God is in charge. Secondly, it takes faith to ask for deliverance when our attention is divided by the storms around us. Peter acknowledges the danger of the storm and shouts for help, after which Jesus delivers him.

What happens when we ask and cry to God for help, and it feels like he is not stretching out his hand to grab us? An anonymous story is told of a young woman who kept complaining to her father how miserable her life was, and that she did not know if or how she was going to make it. It seemed like just as soon as one problem was solved, another quickly followed. Her father, a chef, took her to the kitchen. He filled three pots with water and put them over the fire. When the pots began to boil, he put potatoes in one, eggs in another, and ground coffee beans in the last.

He let them boil for some time then turned off the burners. He took the potatoes out of the pot and placed them in a bowl, the eggs

---

[9] Joanna Adams, "Faith and Fear: 1 John 4:16-19 and Matthew 14:22-33," Journal for Preachers 19, no. 4 (Pentecost 1996): 27.

he put in another bowl, and then he poured the coffee into a cup. He turned to his daughter and asked what she saw. Without any hesitation she said, "Potatoes, eggs and a cup of coffee." He invited her to take a closer look and examine them carefully. She did and noted that the potatoes were soft and the eggs were hard-boiled. Lastly, she picked up the cup of coffee; and even before the first sip, its rich smell brought a smile to her face. "Father, what does this mean?" she asked. Her father explained that the potatoes, eggs and coffee beans had each faced the same adversity–the boiling water. However, each one had reacted differently! The potato went in strong and hard but in boiling water, it became soft and weak. The egg was fragile, with the thin outer shell protecting its interior liquid until it was put into the boiling water. Then the inside of the egg became hard. The coffee however was different; it blended with the water and made itself and the water better. It changed the water and created something new. The father then asked her: "Which one are you, a potato, an egg or a coffee bean? When adversity knocks on your door, how do you respond? Are you a potato, an egg, or a coffee bean?"[10]

Certainly, facing life's difficulties can be worrisome and we can become weak, but the only thing that truly matters is what happens within us. Sometimes we have to face our challenges and believe that God is creating something new in our situation.

Honestly, it is easier to hear that phrase "Do not be afraid" than to truly believe it when we are surrounded by hardship, trauma, uncertainties: fear of death, of physical, spiritual, and emotional pain,

---

[10] (Source: https://www.lakeviewmethodist.org/2016/07/potatoes-eggs-and-coffee- beans/)

of sickness, of injustice, of failure, of losing control and of being controlled, of terrorist attack, of natural disasters, of betrayal, etc., as well as of life itself. All these fears hinder growth and prevent our little faith from functioning. As a result of so much suffering in the world, many people have reasoned that the existence of human suffering cannot be compatible with the existence of a good and powerful God. However, Jesus did not promise us a stress-free life, but he promised to help us carry the burden if we bring it to him: "Come to me all you who are burdened, and I will give you rest….For my yoke is easy and my burden is light" (Mt. 11:28-30).

Conclusion

In reflecting on this Scriptural passage concerning God's actions in our lives, I learned that as Christians, carrying our cross is inevitable, given that suffering is part of life. Although human suffering is not something to be desired, it is sometimes connected to the Paschal mystery experience, and thus becomes a blessing in disguise. However, the hardest element of suffering are the feelings of abandonment, rejection, and the absence of the Divine, which suffering normally evokes in us. This was the experience of the disciples in this passage. Jesus also experienced this abandonment on the cross when he cried out to his Father, "My God, my God, why have you forsaken me?" If Jesus felt abandoned by God, how much more are we to experience it? When such moments come, we should cry out to God to save us.

St. Paul explains: "The message of the cross is foolishness to those who are perishing, but to us who are being saved, it is the power of God" (1 Cor. 1:18). The "message of the cross" is actually a paradox since it is certainly a revelation of that love which infinitely surpasses all human expectations. The cross in and of itself is futile, absurd, and meaningless. However, the cross is embraced for the sake of what was achieved through it.

Furthermore, through the encounter with the Divine nature of Jesus, Peter and the disciples ceased from calling Jesus a ghost, and learned to worship him as the Son of God. On the educational value of suffering, Howard Stone, quoting Soren Kierkegaard, explains that when someone suffers and is willing to learn from it, then one is equally learning about themselves, others, and their relationship with God.[11] This statement is true because the experience of the storms of life connects us with one another and with the Divine. For some people, it is mostly when they are facing hardship that they draw closer to God. Our storms might be overwhelming, but there is always the grace of God. St Paul elucidates: "My grace is sufficient for you, for power is made perfect in weakness. Therefore, I am content with weaknesses, insults, hardships, persecutions, and calamities for the sake of Christ; for whenever I am weak, then I am strong" (2 Cor. 12:9-10).

An African proverb has it that an elephant is not overly burdened by its trunk. In other words, no matter how heavily one suffers, one will not be overburdened by it. The Scripture also explains: "Do not

---

[11] Howard Stone, Theological Context for Pastoral Caregiving: Word in Deed (Binghamton, NY: The Haworth Pastoral Press, Inc., 1996), 136.

disdain the discipline of the Lord, or lose heart when reproved by him; for whom the Lord loves, he disciplines; he scourges every child he acknowledges" (Heb. 12:5-6). The Letter to the Hebrews makes the comparison between God and earthly fathers, in that they both discipline out of love in order to teach important lessons. Although discipline might seem overwhelming at times, nevertheless, the grace of God is always sufficient for our little faith. Thus, to accept human pain as a blessing and an opportunity for growth requires the love and the grace of God to persevere. John Paul II in his Apostolic Letter, Salvifici doloris suggests that love is the answer to the question of the meaning of suffering (S.D 14). Human suffering, though painful, is temporal, potentially good, and fruitful because it unites us with the suffering and resurrection of Christ.

A psychologist, Lionell Corbett, believes that suffering binds us with the cosmos, our concept of the divine, and to each other.[12] This rings true because we are connected to each other and are mutually interdependent beings. No one is an island. The disciples needed the courage of Peter to prove that Jesus was not a ghost. And when Peter shows this courage, they come to the realization that Jesus is truly the Son of God. However, Corbett's argument is not why we suffer, but how we can collectively handle and help a suffering person, especially where the problem is not likely to be resolved and when the suffering is not of one's making. For Corbett, any storm that has no solution should be treated spiritually. With this treatment of suffering in mind, he observes, as he quotes Panikkar, that the concept of

---

[12] Lionell Corbett, The Religious Function of the Psyche (New York, NY: Routledge, 1996), 129.

human suffering is handled differently by different groups as they seek to understand and deal with it. Thus, while "Buddhism seeks to eliminate suffering, Hinduism seeks to deny it, Judaism and Islam seek to explain it, Christianity spiritualizes and transfigures it, and the psychologists psychologize it."[13]

God is a communal and a relational God. Likewise, we are created to be in a relationship with God and with one another. The ultimate good of humanity consists of being in union with God. All other goods or pleasures are secondary. Thus, if this union with God demands carrying the cross or remaining in the storm, so be it! St. Augustine's maxim summarizes it: "Our hearts are restless Oh God, until they rest in you." Jesus did not promise us a cross-free life, but rather he promised to be with us till the end of the age (Mt. 28:20). The knowledge of Jesus' saving power will help us to understand the goodness of God even in the midst of suffering (theodicy). As we journey in the boat of life, the basis of courage for our little faith is the awareness of Jesus' power and his presence in the midst of strife and storm.

---

[13] Corbett, 126.

Chapter 7

RECLAIMING ONE'S PLACE AT THE TABLE

"Sometimes I seek another word to express Love, but in this land of exile the word which begins and ends is quite incapable of rendering the vibrations of the soul; we must then adhere to this simple and only word: TO LOVE."

—St. Thérèse of Lisieux
(Letter to her cousin, Marie Guerin)

Mt. 15:21-28 (NRSV)

21Jesus left that place and went away to the district of Tyre and Sidon. 22Just then a Canaanite woman from that region came out and started shouting, "Have mercy on me, Lord, Son of David; my daughter is tormented by a demon." 23But he did not answer her at all. And his disciples came and urged him, saying, "Send her away, for she keeps shouting after us." 24He answered, "I was sent only to the lost sheep of the house of Israel." 25But she came and knelt before him, saying, "Lord, help me." 26He answered, "It is not fair to take the children's food and throw it to the dogs." 27She said, "Yes, Lord, yet even the dogs eat the crumbs that fall from their masters' table." 28Then Jesus answered her, "Woman, great is your faith! Let it be done for you as you wish." And her daughter was healed instantly.

Introduction

This healing genre appears only in Mark and Matthew. Matthew heavily edited the Marcan version, maybe for theological reasons, since he includes the woman addressing Jesus as Lord and Son of David. Perhaps, this redaction might be as a result of the Sitz im Leben of the Evangelist's community struggling about the acceptance of their Gentile brethren in order to raise both Jews and Gentiles in God's divine plan of salvation.

The passage emphasizes high tension in the Matthean community, who are mostly Jewish Christians, separated from the synagogue, and the power this community has over their Gentile brethren.[1]

The story of the Canaanite woman is very critical and troubling. I have always wondered how the compassionate and caring Jesus seems so prejudiced in this story. Even though Jesus says in Mt 11:6, "Blessed is anyone who takes no offense at me;" I do take offense at Jesus because of this story. Similarly, whenever I have read this healing story before now, my concerns were: why did this woman seemed to be rejected by Jesus and why was she called a dog. Is it because she is a foreigner or because Jesus wants her strong faith to be revealed? Why would Jesus not use another word apart from dog? In my own part of Nigeria, to call someone a dog is very insulting because it denotes that the person sleeps around, i.e., a whore. A dog is not a pet in my culture. The objective of having it in the house is for it to guard

---

[1] Russell Pregeant, Matthew: Chalice Commentaries for Today (St. Louis, MO: Chalice Press, 2004), 124.

the house of the owner A dog sleeps outside or in the house designated for it, and guards the house against any invader.

Consequently, I have tremendous admiration for the faith, courage, humility, and perseverance of the nameless Canaanite woman,
who reclaims her place at the table. Although she tolerated the insult
from Jesus and his disciples, she did not give up. She even worshiped
Jesus, a gesture the disciples lacked at this time.

My goal in reflecting on this passage is to try to understand what
it really means, and how it will help me live a courageous, humble,
and faith- filled life.

Exegesis of Matthew 15:21-28

The territory where the healing occurred is at Tyre and Sidon,
but Matthew locates it in an open space, while Mark's account is in a
house. Even though I am not doing the parallel from Mark, it is good
to mention the significant differences. Mark writes that the Canaanite woman is a Greek and a Syro-phoenician by birth, while Matthew
writes that the woman is a Canaanite. What is the relationship between the two areas? Why is Jesus in Gentile territory when he had
warned his disciples earlier (Mt 10:5-6) not to enter the Gentile
town, but rather to go to the lost sheep of Israel? This reference seems
a contradictory statement to Jesus' final words to his followers to go
and make disciples of all nations in 28:19. It may be that at this time
the appointed time to evangelize the foreigners has not come. However, the Canaanite woman would not wait for this appointed time;
she approaches Jesus just like the Centurion did.

Jesus had gone into the region of Tyre and Sidon. This is her home. Matthew's choice of the word "Canaanite" seems a bit strange. By the time of Jesus, Gentiles were no longer called "Canaanites." According to Adrian Leske, Canaanite is a term that appears outdated because the inhabitants of the land had disappeared. In Deuteronomy 7:1-6, God commanded the Israelites to exterminate the Canaanites lest the Israelites have contact with them especially through marriage and commit idolatry. However, the Greek traders who are occupying the land at that time are despised by the Jews because of their unethical trade practices.[2] Thus, the region is economically comfortable.

Additionally, "Canaanite" is a derogatory name used by the Jews for the Gentiles. It is probably the reason why Luke does not include this healing story in his Gospel. Even though Matthew and Luke use Mark as their source, one would not expect Luke, a Gentile, to use a derogatory term for himself and his audience.

Matthew's story may be evidence that the Canaanites were not wiped out but continue to live among the Israelites (Jgs 1:27-33). Mark is thus correct in calling the woman a Greek, since the Greeks occupied the land then. Matthew, on the other hand, is not wrong to call her a Canaanite woman since the Matthean community is a Jewish community. Perhaps Matthew uses the term to intensify the contrast between the "pious" Jewish leaders whom Jesus had just

---

[2] Adrian Leske, "Matthew," in The International Bible Commentary: A Catholic and Ecumenical Commentary for the Twenty-first Century, ed. William Farmer et al., (Collegeville, MN: The Liturgical Press, 1998), 1301.

condemned in 15:1-20 and the outstanding faith of this Gentile woman.[3] This implies that it is neither observing Jewish cultic practices, nor being a Gentile that automatically makes one a member of the fictive kinship of which Jesus is the head, but rather faith in Him. Thus, the first part of chapter 15 explains what defiles the heart, and the second part confirms that the heart is healed through faith in Jesus.[4]

This healing story might also portray the difficulty the Matthean Jewish community is facing before they welcomed Gentiles into their community. Are they to be circumcised first and follow the Torah, or are they to be admitted on the basis of their faith in Jesus Christ? Examples of this dilemma are seen by the incident recorded in Acts of the Apostles during the Council at Jerusalem, pertaining to the conditions needing to be met before admitting the Gentiles into Christianity (Acts 15), as well as Peter's experience before converting Cornelius (Acts 10:9-16). In the Matthean community, the kingdom of God is related to justice, and justice goes hand in hand with mission.[5] Consequently, accepting Gentiles into their community is being just, thus fulfilling Jesus' final word to proclaim the gospel to all nations. For Jesus makes it clear that he has other sheep that do not belong to their fold which must be brought into the fold in order to have one Shepherd and one flock (Jn. 10:16).

---

[3] Leske, 1301.

[4] Frederick Bruner, Matthew: A Commentary, Vol. 2, revised and expanded edition (Grand Rapids, MI: William B. Eerdmans, 2004), 97.

[5] Johannes Nissen, "Matthew, Mission, and Method," International Review of Mission 91, no. 360 (Jan 2002): 79.

In order for Jesus to gather this flock, he leaves the place where he has been admonishing the Pharisees because of their cultic practices (washing of hands before eating) and goes to the district of Tyre and Sidon. Even though the reason for Jesus' going away is not indicated in Matthew's gospel, one might wonder whether he desires to be alone or whether he is escaping the persecution of his enemies after his strong condemnation of their traditions.[6] It is also surprising to see Jesus in Gentile territory since he had warned his disciples not to enter a Gentile town. Perhaps he is now willing to share his Messianic blessings with the Gentiles. According to Amy-Jill Levine, this healing and that of the Centurion's servant are the only two healings concerning the Gentiles and are accomplished from a distance. Levine continues that the healings demonstrate that the Gentiles are also worthy of Jesus' healing and they will eventually receive the gospel.[7]

In Matthew's account, the healing takes place in a public setting outside the institutional setting, i.e., Temple or synagogue. The woman comes to meet Jesus in an open space since it is clear that Jesus was in her territory. This is contrary to Mark's account that depicts Jesus in a house. How did she know of Jesus' identity? Perhaps the traders mentioned above, who moved in and out of Tyre, carried home the news about Jesus and his miracles (active gossip network).

---

[6] Rudolf Schnackenburg, The Gospel of Matthew, trans. Robert Barr (Grand Rapids, MI: William B. Eerdmans Company, 2002), 150.

[7] Amy-Jill Levine, "Matthew," in Women's Bible Commentary, Expanded edition with Apocrypha, eds. Carol Newsom and Sharon Ringe (Louisville, KY: Westminster John Knox Press, 1998), 346.

The woman's "coming out" might also be symbolic of her leaving her pagan worship to embrace the religion of Jesus.[8] Basically, in Matthean community, doing a mission is not only going out to evangelize, but it also involves Gentiles coming to worship, just like the story of the Magi.

Leske suggests that the woman may have been a widow since she has no sponsor.[9] No wonder she goes alone to meet Jesus in a society characterized by community solidarity, where women are not valued. The Canaanite woman's oikos—household—must have suffered from shame because of the condition of her daughter. She becomes a broker for her daughter (even though Jesus is the primary broker who works through the power of God—the Patron), and at the same time she becomes a client seeking Jesus' help to restore the honor of her household.

Furthermore, both Jesus and the Canaanite woman are in need. Jesus' day up to that point had been frustrating, and he needs to rest after confronting the Jewish people to whom he was sent, and who had subsequently rejected him. The woman is also in great need, and struggles to get his attention. She alone bears the burden of truly knowing the anguish that her daughter is enduring.

The woman addresses Jesus as "Lord," and "Son of David." It is astonishing to see a non-Jew address Jesus as "Lord" and "Son of David." Her proclamation shows that Jesus' fame has gone beyond

---

[8]   John Nolland, "'Have Mercy on Me': The Story of the Canaanite Woman in Matthew 15:21-28," Journal of Theological Studies, Vol. 55, no. 1 (April 2004): 235.

[9] Leske, 1301.

Jewish territory. Levine sees this proclamation as the "woman's acknowledgment of the priority of the Jews in the divine plan of salvation."[10] The Canaanite woman's voice is that of a disciple when many Jewish people reject this conviction. Her words of address echo those of the blind men (9:27), and emphasize Matthew's aim to depict Jesus as the Messiah, the Son of David, and the Son of Abraham. The woman addresses Jesus as Lord three times (a significant number), thus acknowledging Jesus' superiority.

Nevertheless, it is shocking to watch Jesus rebuff the woman in spite of her proclamation of faith. As readers, we expect Jesus to respond immediately as he has been doing in his ministry. It is also applicable to our prayer life, we expect God to answer our prayers straight away. But how often do we ignore beggars on our way? How often are we insensitive to the cry of our neighbors? Perhaps, Jesus is trying to see whether her proclamations are from her heart or probably the human and Jewish Jesus is manifesting in this passage.

The disciples viewed her as a nuisance and maybe judged her based on her race, gender, or both.[11] They request Jesus to send her away. That is exactly what they did in the chapter before this section, in the story where they were faced with a hungry crowd of over 5,000 that needed to be fed. "Send the crowds away," the disciples said to Jesus. Jesus responded: "You give them something to eat," (Mt. 14:15-16). Most likely they don't wish to associate with a Gentile, or maybe

---

[10] Ibid.

[11] Kerry Dearborn, "Matthew" in The IVP Women's Bible Commentary, ed. Catherine Kroeger and Mary Evans (Downers Grove, IL: Inter Varsity Press, 2002), 534.

they wanted Jesus to grant her request and then send her away. Even though she has become a bother, this Canaanite woman isn't going anywhere. Just like the blind men in Mt. 9:27, she calls out to Jesus and also uses the language of the Jewish prayer: "Have mercy on me, Lord, Son of David."

Very unlike him, Jesus is not moved by this prayerful request. Rather he responded: "I am sent only to the lost sheep of the house of Israel." It is not clear whom Jesus is directing this response to. Two petitions are made: from the woman and from the disciples, yet Jesus does not respond to either of them. Perhaps he is confirming his earlier instruction to the disciples in 10:6, to go only to the lost sheep of the house of Israel. However, it is encouraging that Jesus didn't say that he is not sent to the Gentiles, but that he was sent first to the Israelites. Bruner maintains that just as Jesus struggles to understand his mission, so also the woman struggles to find Jesus' help. The two struggles are interrelated since the woman will not find His help, until Jesus finds the will of his Father.[12]

Accordingly, the woman's struggle to find Jesus' help causes her to persevere in soliciting for her daughter's healing. She won't give up! To demonstrate that she actually knows who Jesus is, she kneels before him and cries even more. "Lord, help me," she begs. Her kneeling is another gesture of humility, of social inferiority, and that of a client seeking favor from a patron.[13] Thus, she acknowledges the

---

[12] Bruner, 101.

[13] Adaku H. Ogbuji, Dealing Effectively with Domestic Abuse: The Ministry of Reconciliation and Healing (Nairobi, Kenya: CUEA Press, 2015), 116.

social inequality between Jesus and herself. His response, "it is not fair to take the children's food and throw it to the dogs," is not only negative, but also outrageous and deeply offensive. Bruner writes that the word for dog used here is a house or domestic dog (diminutive form) as opposed to a wild dog. The Greek word for it is kunarios which means "little dogs or puppies."[14] Does it really matter the kind of dog Jesus meant— puppy or wild dog? The fact remains that Jesus' response is a dreadfully racial insult and extremely discriminating.

Michael Fallon suggests that the remark might be a traditional anti-Gentile proverb common among Jews which even the woman understood.[15] Matthew used the notion of dogs in 7:6, when he asserts that one should not give what is holy to dogs. What is holy might be food for children, which is not given to puppies. Scott Martin, in interpreting these words, believes that Jesus is simply rude to this woman and fails the test of good manners. He continues that the woman and her compatriots should not have to go through such denigration before her request is granted.[16] But why is Jesus hesitant to grant the woman's appeal even after she kneels before him? Could it be the human Jesus responding and reflecting his religious and cultural prejudice?

---

[14] Bruner, 101.

[15] Michael Fallon, The Gospel According to Matthew: An Introductory Commentary (Bangalore, India: Asian Trading Corporation, 2002), 223.

[16] Scott Martin, "Matthew 15:21-28: A Test-case for Jesus' Manners," Journal for the Study of the New Testament, no. 63 (September 1996): 43-44.

Interestingly, it is possible that Jesus, as a faithful Jew, prayed the prayer of the Jews; i.e. thanking God that he was born a Jew not a Gentile; and also a man and not a woman. It is surprising to note that his hesitancy in this passage is the total opposite of his immediate willingness to go to the house of the Centurion to heal his servant in 8:5-17 who also happened to be a Gentile.

But the Canaanite woman is persistent and determined, she did not walk away. The life of her daughter is at stake. If she had gone away, it might actually confirm that she came up as a dog. She paraphrases Jesus' words and responds with courage: "Yes, Lord, yet even the dogs eat the crumbs that fall from their masters' table." With this statement, she faithfully welcomes Jesus' humiliation and recognizes Israel's precedence in the economy of salvation as well as the Gospel going beyond Israel. Although she intends to get the crumbs, which would be life-giving since they were from the Lord, she however, gets the real food. This is an act of faith which Jesus commends: "Woman, great is your faith."

In fact, her faith is a reminder of the other faithful Gentile women in the genealogy of Jesus, such as Tamar, Rahab, and Ruth.[17] For even those who eat at the table with Jesus still doubt whether this carpenter's son could truly be the Messiah. The food, which many translations refer to as bread, is symbolic. It might be considered a symbol of salvation, e.g., the feeding stories. The table might be considered the symbol of the Lord's Table—the Eucharist (1Cor 10:21). With the woman's response, Jesus for once, loses his argument and

---

[17] Joe Kapolyo, "Matthew," in African Bible Commentary, ed. Tokunboh Adeyemo et al., (Nairobi, Kenya: Wordalive Publishers, 2006), 1142.

opens up to the "other," the "stranger," and to the "different," as well as to who He is—Son of God. He embraces the challenge and changes to the radical inclusion of everyone. It was a moment of intercultural conversion for Jesus. He comes to a new awareness of his mission and the wider vision of the kingdom of God. Jesus saw and heard a fuller revelation of God in the voice and face of the Canaanite woman. Thus, despite emphasizing the priority of feeding the children of Israel, he could not ignore the pleas of a mother for her sick child.

Towards the end of this chapter, there is also the feeding story of 4000 men besides women and children, which ended with seven baskets of leftover food. Matthew placed the story of Jesus and the Canaanite woman between these two feeding stories. The Canaanite woman taught Jesus that she and her daughter deserve more than crumbs. They deserved also to be fed at the table. And if Jesus does not feed them, it will contribute to their oppression. Ultimately, Jesus did not only feed them, but also healed and welcomed them to his fictive kinship.

This is in contrast with the faithlessness of the self-righteous religious leaders whom Jesus reprimanded because of their hypocrisy before this healing genre, who, although being children of Israel and eating from the table, do not have faith in Jesus. The disciples of Jesus are also faithless; Jesus had to rebuke them as people of little faith in 16:8-12 and 8:26. Thus, the Canaanite woman is honored in her willingness to eat the crumbs. Her humility buys her a seat at the table. These Scripture texts go a long way to illustrate that God has a preference for the needy, the oppressed, and the poor. God can even change his mission in order to address the needs of the weak. Finally, with this healing story, Matthew is reminding his community as well as all Christians, that both Jews and Gentiles must approach the Table of Christ with faith.

Conclusion

What can we learn from the story of the Canaanite woman? She heard so many discouraging voices: from Jesus (she is called a dog) and from the disciples, (send her away) but she didn't give in to negativity. Sometimes so many discouraging voices fill our ears and mind. Other times people make our business theirs and tell us what to do. While it is good to listen to wise advice, the end decision is ours to make. This reminded me of a fable told by Aesop, who lived in the 6th Century, about listening to several voices.

Once there was a man and his son who were leading their donkey in order to market to sell it. As they walked along the road, two men going the other way passed them and said: "Fools! What is wrong with you? You have a donkey, why aren't you riding on it?" So, the man put his son on the donkey and went on. Soon they passed another group of men and one of them said: "What a spoiled boy. His weak father walks while he gets to ride." So, the man decided to lift the boy off and got on to ride. The boy led the donkey with his father riding until they came to a group of women who said to them: "Shame on this lazy and insensitive man, riding on the donkey while that poor boy is forced to walk several miles." So the man lifted his son on the donkey and they both rode it down the road. Then they came to some men sitting along the road, who began to berate the father and son saying: "Aren't you ashamed of overloading that poor donkey with both of you on its back in this hot sun?" They both got off and went down the road a short distance wondering what to do. They decided to cut a pole, tie the donkey's feet to it and putting the pole on their shoulders carried the donkey down the road. As they passed by, another crowd jeered at them for carrying the donkey rather than riding on it. When they got to the bridge, the donkey got a foot loose and in the struggle fell off the bridge into the river where it drowned and died.[18]

Whose voice do we hear or listen to? Do we carry these voices and allow them to hinder our growth? Remember that you cannot please everyone. No matter what you do, someone will always find something negative to say. Others judge and criticize people when they are not happy with their own lives. Do not carry your donkey with a pole. You don't need people's approval to be happy.

The Canaanite woman did not listen to the discouraging voices and prejudices. She is a role model for those who have faced humiliation, ethnocentric bias, racial discrimination, abuse of every kind, and those women and children who have been trafficked and sold into slavery for sexual gain in many parts of the world; victims of war who have been raped, and refugees who have been molested. In the face of adversity and rejection, we are to stand firm and be courageous, so that we could walk in the shoes of this brave woman. She

---

[18] Paul Luvera, "Lessons from the Man, his Son and the Donkey," (Retrieved from https://plaintifftriallawyertips.com/lessons-from-the-man-his-son-the-donkey).

never allowed her situation to cloud her sense of reasoning. She did however, challenge the status quo by bravely meeting Jesus. It might not be lawful for a non-Jew, especially a woman, to approach a Jew in a public place, but she did.

In the first place, Jesus takes the initiative of moving to the Gentile's territory. Certainly, Jesus' going there is not an accident, there is a purpose in it. If he had wanted to rest, he could have gone up the mountain as he would normally do. He intends to bring the kingdom of God to them also. Similarly, Jesus comes to us every day. Thus, we are challenged to get up and meet him as the nameless Canaanite woman did.

In reflecting on these Biblical texts, I realized that it is challenging to understand how God works. Indeed, God's ways are not our ways (Is 55:8-9). We have to be patient with God and allow His will to be done at the appropriate time. It is also apparent that Jesus' love is limitless and immeasurable to both Jews and non-Jews alike. Jesus never abandons those who trust in him. It might be delayed but it will never be denied. When God tests us (Ps 11:5) as the Canaanite woman was tested, we are to stand firm and persevere.

It is also vivid in the passage that the Matthean community is not perfect, but rather a community of Jewish Christians battling with pharisaic intra- group conflict. Their major problems are: how to incorporate the Gentile Christians into their community and also how they could live a fulfilling Christian life even as they struggled with their Jewish traditions. These two problems are clearly seen in chapter fifteen of Matthew's Gospel. It is also clear from the texts that the Matthean community was not an egalitarian community. Jewish

Christians are presented as children, who are superior to the Gentile Christians. Why is the Matthean community not an egalitarian community given that they are of one flock and under one Shepherd? Why does the evangelist use two different measuring rods with the healing of the centurion's servant and the healing of the Canaanite woman's daughter, although both are Gentiles and both have strong faith in Jesus? Why is this mission to the Gentiles initially a controversy? At first, the mission was only to "the lost sheep of Israel," and later, to "all nations." What might be the reaction of the conservative Jewish Christians to the universal mission mandate in 28:19-20, since it entails turning to the Gentiles and consequently, a total separation from Judaism and its traditions? This mandate is the summary of the Gospel of Matthew's course—Jesus' movement from the Jewish territory to the Gentile's territory. This movement is a huge transition and Jesus' aim might be to institute the universal mission mandate, which he will hand over to his disciples before he ascends to heaven.

Another incident that is related to the Gospel of Matthew's course in this Scripture story is the confession of faith of the Canaanite Woman; "Have mercy on me, Lord, Son of David." With this profession of faith, she acknowledges Jesus as the expected Messiah, which the Evangelist aimed at proving throughout his Gospel; that Jesus is the Christ (Messiah), the son of Abraham and the son of David (Mt 1:1).

Lastly, another area this pericope is related to the Gospel of Matthew's course is the fact that faith in Jesus makes one a member of the household (oikos) of God. Faith in Jesus facilitates the Canaanite woman's membership to the fictive kinship headed by Jesus, as well as her ability to reclaim her place at the table.

Chapter 8

THE IMPARTIALITY OF GOD:
A PAULINE EMPHASIS IN ROMANS 2:12-24

"How shall I show my love is proved by deeds? No other means have I of proving my love than to do the very least actions and do them for Love."

—St. Thérèse of Lisieux (*Story of a Soul*)

Romans 2:12-24 (NRSV)

12All who have sinned apart from the law will also perish apart from the law, and all who have sinned under the law will be judged by the law. 13For it is not the hearers of the law who are righteous in God's sight, but the doers of the law who will be justified. 14When Gentiles, who do not possess the law, do instinctively what the law requires, these, though not having the law, are a law to themselves. 15They show that what the law requires is written on their hearts, to which their own conscience also bears witness; and their conflicting thoughts will accuse or perhaps excuse them 16on the day when, according to my gospel, God, through Jesus Christ, will judge the secret thoughts of all. 17But if you call yourself a Jew and rely on the law and boast of your relation to God 18and know his will and determine what is best because you are instructed in the law, 19and if you are sure that you are a guide to the blind, a light to those who are in darkness, 20a corrector of the foolish, a teacher of children, having in the law the embodiment of knowledge and truth, 21you, then, that teach others, will you not teach yourself? While you preach against stealing, do you steal? 22You that forbid adultery, do you commit adultery? You that abhor idols, do you rob temples? 23You that boast in the law, do you dishonor God by breaking the law? 24For, as it is written, "The name of God is blasphemed among the Gentiles because of you."

Introducing the Roman Christian Community

The letter to the Romans is an extensive and persuasive letter which Paul wrote to a church that he did not establish. This letter probably served as a self-presentation letter and an avenue to introduce himself to the Roman Christians because he had planned to visit them on his way to Spain after delivering proceeds from Macedonia and Achaia to Jerusalem (Rm 15:22-29). There is no exact agreement among scholars when this letter was written. Joseph Fitzmyer believes Paul wrote it around AD 57-58.[1] Brendan Byrne fixes it in the winter of any year between AD 54 and early AD 59.[2] On the other hand, Jerome Murphy-O'Connor thinks that Paul wrote it around AD 55-56.[3]

However, there is some evidence that Paul wrote this letter before his trip to Jerusalem (15:25), after evangelizing in Illyricum (15:19),

---

[1] Joseph A. Fitzmyer, "The Letter to the Romans," in The New Jerome Biblical Commentary, ed.Raymond Brown, Joseph Fitzmyer, and Roland Murphy (Englewood Cliff, NJ: Prentice Hall, 1990), 830.

[2] Brendan Byrne, Roman, Sacra Pagina Series, Vol. 6, ed. Harrington Daniel (Collegeville, MN: Liturgical Press, 1996), 9.

[3] Jerome Murphy-O'Connor, Paul: A Critical Life (Oxford, NY: Oxford University Press, 1996), 323.

Macedonia, and Achaia (15:26). Paul most likely wrote it in Cench-rea[4] or in Corinth where he was hosted by Gaius (16:23) through Tertius, perhaps dictating the letter to him (16:22).

Paul actually wished to visit the Christians in Rome (1:11, 13) since their faith resounded all over the world (1:7, 8), thus he wrote an ambassadorial letter[5] to introduce himself and his office to the church. This letter would in effect stand for him or represent him just like an ambassador represents a state. These Christians may not have known Paul or even shared some of his theological views, so it's no wonder that this letter of introduction has the clearest exposition of why Paul wrote it. It is not very clear the makeup of Paul's audience; likely he was writing to Torah-observant Christians, although there might be Gentile Christians in Rome (1:13, 11:13). Hence, Paul used a diplomatic and Septuagint language, which Torah-observant Christians would understand, in order to establish a common ground and reach out to them. An example of this language was Paul's play with words in explaining Jesus' Divinity and humanity in 1:2-4; e.g., "spirit of holiness" instead of Holy Spirit, as well as "who was descended from David according to the flesh." Here Paul used flesh to depict Jesus' humanity unlike how he used it in other letters as something opposed to the spirit (Gal 5:16-21).

Paul used a diplomatic speech—paralipsis—in explaining to the church his reason for writing them. According to Paul, the letter was not actually for conversion reasons since the Christians could

---

[4] Fitzmyer, "The Letter to the Romans," 830.

[5] Klaus Haacker, New Testament Theology: The Theology of Paul's Letter to the Romans (New York, NY: Cambridge University Press, 2003), 22.

instruct themselves, but rather to remind them of the gospel which was held in common (15:14-15). Although Paul claimed that this letter was not for conversion reasons, the letter intended to bring people to faith in Jesus Christ. Charles Puskas held the view that the letter to the Romans promoted doctrinal harmony, ecclesiastical solidarity, and Christian hospitality[6] as Paul hoped that the church in Rome would support his mission in Spain.

Because the founder of the Roman Christian community remained unknown, it is possible that Jewish Christians evangelized the Romans.[7] Byrne thinks that the economic and religious contacts between Jerusalem and Rome must have facilitated the establishment of the Roman church.[8] Evidence is seen in Acts 2:10 where visitors from Rome witnessed the Pentecost experience of the Apostles. These visitors might be Jews in Diaspora who were fulfilling the temple service laws by visiting Jerusalem three times a year. In addition, the Roman church was organized around home churches (16:5), and the majority of its members were lower class people, slaves and freedpersons,[9] as well as those with property since some had homes to host church members. Because the church in Rome did not have an

---

[6] Charles Puskas, The Letters of Paul: An Introduction (Collegeville, MN: The Liturgical Press, 1993), 83.

[7] Murphy-O'Connor, 333.

[8] Byrne, 10.

[9] Ibid., 11.

apostolic foundation, the house churches had no centralized author-ity structure.[10]

This reflection tries to discover Paul's mission, his persuasive agenda, and his theological preoccupations to the Christians in Rome as he argues that God is fair to all people both Jews and Gentiles.

Exegesis of Romans 2:12-24

As one would expect, the letter to the Romans has the standard structure which characterizes Paul's letters—opening greetings, a thanksgiving, the body of the letter, and closing remarks. The opening part mentions Paul as the sender. The addressees are the beloved of God in Rome and Paul imparts the Jewish priestly blessing, "Grace to you and peace from God our Father." This opening remark is followed by a thanksgiving, commending the church for their steadfastness in faith. The body of the letter deals with the mission Paul is determined to achieve. It contains admonition and doctrinal issues, in order to solve some of the problems that the church was facing. It starts with the question of faith and Paul rebuking the Gentiles for worshipping images rather than God (1:18- 23); Paul also confirms God's wrath against the offenders.

In chapter two, Paul's attention turns towards the Torah-observant Christians. He addresses four issues: the supposed

---

[10] Ben Witherington III and Darlene Hyatt, Paul's Letter to the Romans: A Socio- Rhetorical Commentary (Grand Rapids, MI: William B. Eerdmans Publishers, 2004), 9.

superiority of the Jews (v 1-11), the Possession of the Torah (12-16), Jewish national privilege (17-24), and circumcision (25-29). The central message is that both Jews and Gentiles stand in need of the redemptive work of God done through Jesus Christ, which is made accessible by faith in Jesus. Although the Jews appear to have several advantages over the Gentiles, God treats both equally since he shows no partiality (2:11). Finally, the letter ends with concluding remarks, traveling plans, and final blessings. As mentioned above the composition of Paul's audience is not very clear; thus, the identity of those outside of the law, and those under the law is also unclear. Are those outside of the law Gentile Christians or pagans and are those under the law Christian Jews? However, since Paul praises his audience for their faith which resounds all over the world, we might assume that they are Christians who are called to be saints (1:7). In verse 12, Paul argues that possession of the law is irrelevant since those who sinned outside of the law will perish outside of the law; at the same time, those who sinned under the law will be judged by the law. It suggests that no one will be exempted from the judgment of God since He will deal with both Jews and Gentiles according to where they are. The Jews will be judged with the law since they are privileged to have it, to know God's will through the law, and be able to discern what is essential on the basis of the law.[11] The Gentiles (who are outside of the Law) will receive their own judgment outside of the law.

Basically, what is necessary for eschatological justification is doing what the law requires—but the doers of the law will be justified. Paul echoes the words of Leviticus 18:5 which affirm that all those

---

[11] Haacker, 97.

who keep the law shall live and not only hearers of the law. Joseph Fitzmyer explains that Paul uses nomos (law) in many ways: in a generic sense as law (Gal 5:23), in a figurative sense as a principle (3:27a), as a way of referring to sin (7:23c), as human nature (2:14d), as the Old Testament (3:19), but most of the time as the Law of Moses (14:34).[12] In this pericope, when Paul writes about the law, he is referring to the Torah.

There is evidence in vs. 13 of internal struggles over the law between the Torah-observant Christians and the Gentile Christians. Perhaps, Paul was accused by the Jewish Christians of nullifying the law. N. T. Wright argues that Paul might be responding to an implied Jewish utterance; "We at least have Torah."[13]

Apparently, Paul is aware of this internal struggle that some Jewish Christians are boasting of being in possession of the law. Thus, the Gentiles were either encouraged or persuaded to observe the works of the law. Paul is also conscious of the position of the Jews on the basis of their covenant with God, and the preferential treatment they enjoyed in respect to God's judgment. The Jewish expectation about God is described well in the Wisdom of Solomon: "So while chastening us, you scourge our enemies ten thousand times more, so that, when we judge, we may meditate upon your goodness, and when we are judged, we may expect mercy" (Ws 12:22). For Paul to

---

[12] Joseph Fitzmyer, Paul and His Theology: A Brief Sketch, 2nd ed. (Englewood Cliffs, NJ: Prentice Hall, 1989), 75.

[13] N. T. Wright, "The Letter to the Romans," in The New Interpreter's Bible, Vol X, ed. Leander E. Keck et al (Nashville, TN: Abingdon Press, 2002), 440.

convince his audience on the impartiality of God, he explained that each person would be judged on an individual basis since God would repay each according to one's deeds (2:6). It is no longer a question of belonging to the covenantal race, knowing the Torah, or having access to the God of Abraham, but rather, it is a question of having an individual relationship with God and by putting faith in Jesus Christ. Thus, a true Christian is one who is circumcised in the heart (2:29).

Since Paul preaches the gospel of Jesus, who did not come to abolish the law, Paul is never against the Law. However, Paul is convinced that the love of neighbor fulfills all laws (13:8-10). Paul's theology of the law in vs. 13 sounds positive; it is the same in vs. 7:12, "The law is holy and the commandment is holy, just, and good." On the other hand, in 3:20, Paul emphasizes that no one would be justified in the sight of God by deeds prescribed by the law, because through the law comes the knowledge of sin, but one is justified through faith in Jesus. Incidentally, the latter statement, that we are justified through faith in Jesus, does not contradict the former since those who walk in the Spirit fulfill the law, not according to the flesh but rather according to the Spirit (8:4).

Justification (dikaiosyne) is used by Paul to express the effects of the Christ event—passion, death, and resurrection.[14] For Paul to say that the doers of the law will be justified does not have literal meaning. Justification here means reaching the apex of friendship with God. It means righteousness, justice, love, rightness, rectitude, and moral uprightness. Paul talks about justification as a goal already

---

[14] Fitzmyer, *Paul and his Theology*, 59.

achieved. The theology behind this argument is that observing what the law commands without acts of justice and love cannot bring salvation. Justification comes by grace as a gift through faith in Jesus.

Accordingly, the ultimate justification is faith in Jesus Christ, since the law does not give life. The law was supposed to give life (Lev 18:5), but since it could not give life, God sent his Son who brought life to the world (8:3). Therefore, it is the Christ-events that provide justification not the law. Paul explains it clearly that: "If justification comes through the law, then Christ died for nothing" (Galatians 2:21). Likewise, John Cobb expresses that the law was given to deal with sin before Christ's victory over the power of sin. Thus, to rely on the law after this victory is to deny the reality of the Christ-event.[15] The gospel which Paul proclaims is that justification is by faith in Jesus Christ whose salvific act redeems, and it is necessary for all people both Gentiles and Jews. For Paul, being in possession of the Torah need not lead to boasting, since the requirements of it have not been lived up to by some of the same Jews that are boasting about them.

What about the Gentiles? How can they be saved without the Torah? In vs. 14, Paul tries to answer these rhetorical questions. Paul answers that although the Gentiles do not possess the law, they still observe what it requires since the law is written in their hearts. This explains why the Gentiles without the knowledge of Mosaic Law will also be punished because their conscience would bear witness against them. In this phrase, "When gentiles, who do not possess the

---

[15] John Cobb and David Lull, Romans, Chalice Commentaries for Today (St. Louis, MO: Chalice Press, 2005), 62.

law," Paul is not referring to all the Gentiles, but only those who do not have the law, and yet instinctively know the moral values to be observed. If they are Christians, why would they do by nature what the law requires instead of through the Spirit? It might be evidence that these Gentiles are pagans. Later in 8:4, Paul employed his usual tradition of fulfilling the law in the Spirit rather than in the flesh.

The phrase, do instinctively or by nature what the law requires, means that these Gentiles do not observe the entire law, but that their moral behavior counteracts the exaggerated claim made for the law that it is the only moral guide.[16] At least the Gentiles are a law to themselves and do not have to go through the process of studying the requirements of the law like their Jewish counterparts since the Gentiles spontaneously perform the requirements of the law by their own free will. Räisänen argues that Paul's declaration that Gentiles are law to themselves contradicts his initial statement that the Gentiles are without law.[17] On the other hand, Fitzmyer observes that the Gentiles are a law to themselves because they have in them physis (natural order of things) as a guide for their conduct.[18] Paul might be quoting Jeremiah's prophecy of the new covenant when God would inscribe the law in the hearts of his people (Jer 31:33). Apparently, the new covenant has been sealed in Jesus, and all the believers are gifted with the grace of the Spirit of God, so the Gentiles who receive Jesus become a law to themselves.

---

[16] Byrne, 89.
[17] Räisänen, 104.
[18] Ibid.

In vs. 15, Paul argues that God being impartial, will not judge Gentile sinners from the proceedings of the Torah apart from the one written in their hearts, to which their conscience bear witness. Paul's word for conscience is syneidēsis.[19] It is by means of the conscience that the Gentiles performed some of the requirements of the law. Maybe Paul is not arguing for natural law, but rather criticizing the impression of the ethnic superiority of the Jews. Interestingly, Paul makes it clear that having the law is not a guarantee that one is doing what the law requires and also it is not a protection against God's judgment when the law is disobeyed. The Gentiles, at the same time, cannot escape from judgment since their consciences reprimand them when they sinned. Thus, the Gentiles are no worse off because they did not have the Torah. While the Gentiles have a moral obligation to their consciences, the Torah- observant Christians also have an obligation to obey their consciences which have been informed by the Torah.

Furthermore, vs. 16 has an eschatological note: "On that day." Here Paul might be referring to the second coming of Christ because he was convinced that Christ would return very soon (1 Thess. 5:1-11). Many scholars have observed that vs.16 seems to be specifically Christian, and some see it as an interpolation,[20] or maybe a gloss introduced into the text.[21] Paul's rhetorical statements suggest that there are two sets of Gentiles and Jews: those who obey the

---

[19] Fitzmyer Joseph, "Pauline Theology," in The New Jerome Biblical Commentary, 1414.

[20] Lamp, 49.

[21] Byrne, 94.

requirements of the law, either written in their hearts or on a tablet, and those who do not obey the law. Both groups will be judged by an impartial God through Jesus Christ on that day. The argument that all will be judged through Jesus Christ indicates that neither the Torah nor natural law is adequate for redemption, but rather faith in Jesus. Paul mentions a phrase— according to my gospel—that also occurs in chapter 16:25 and in 2 Tim 2:8; however, it might be that Paul is suggesting that his proclamation comes from Jesus and it is in accordance with the gospel of Christ which is the power of God for salvation, to everyone who has faith.

While Vs. 14 -16 are mainly for Gentiles, vs. 17-24 present an admonition for Jews who belonged to the Roman church. "But if you call yourself a Jew and boast of your relation to God." During Paul's time, it might be that Christians perceived themselves as Jews, either by virtue of ethnic heritage, or by the reading of the Hebrew Scriptures, the Torah and the Prophets. Thus, they came to accept Jesus as the long awaited Messiah. Therefore, Paul's phrase "but if you call yourself a Jew" is not an objection to Judaism since he is referring to Christians. Wright surmises that Paul is not admonishing or accusing all the Jews, but rather an individual,[22] hence Paul addresses him in a second person singular. The name "a Jew" was given to the individual indicating his/her privileged status as a chosen child of God. Later in vs. 29, Paul would define a true Jew as one who is circumcised spiritually in the heart.

The word boast, is very common and frequently used by Paul. But the usage here is pejorative since the Jewish interlocutor in the

---

[22] Wright, 445.

Roman church boasted of having been a Jew, of his relationship with God, of his access to the Torah, and of his having been instructed in the law. Paul does not refute his Jewish identity; however Paul is concerned that his boasting ought to be rooted in God. "Let the one who boasts, boast in the Lord" (1 Cor 1:31, 2 Cor 10:17). Thus, the kind of boasting that Paul commends is boasting in the Lord since salvation is the act of God through Jesus.

The phrase, because you are instructed in the law, shows that every Jew was catechized on the precepts of the law so as to observe them. For instance, the young Jesus in Luke 2:46 had been found in the Temple learning and asking questions. Paul himself studied the law under Gamaliel (Acts 22:3). He was zealous for the law and defended it at all costs. Among the Jews, the Torah is supreme because it defines their character, trains and educates them. Consequently, the knowledge of the law is the basis of knowing God and having a relationship with Him. Hence, the law is defended even to the point of death. Because of their knowledge of the law, the Jews were to be light to those in darkness, guide the blind, correct the foolish, and teach the children. Here Paul describes the Gentiles using the terms—darkness, blind, foolish, and children.

Are the Gentiles actually without knowledge like children and fools when the requirements of the law are written in their hearts? Maybe they are not; nevertheless, Paul is pointing out their vulnerability, and how the bearers of the solution, became part of the problem. In other words, the Jews who were supposed to be a light to guide the Gentile Christians in their Roman church failed in that duty. Wright describes it well in this metaphor "A doctor, instead of healing the sick has been infected with the disease."[23]

In this question: You, then, who teach others, will you not teach yourself? Paul was not in opposition to some Jews who were teaching the Gentiles the truth and knowledge of the law, but his concern was the inconsistency of not practicing what the law required. These devout Jews were contradicting their roles as guides, teachers, instructors, and possessors of the embodiment of the knowledge of truth of the law. Earlier in 2:1, Paul had condemned those who judged others because they committed the same offense they were judging. Now in vs. 21 Paul addresses the hypocritical life or failure to practice what one has instructed others to do. This is similar to Jesus' advice to his disciples and the crowd: "Do whatever the Pharisees teach you, but do not do what they do, because the Pharisees do not practice what they teach" (Mt. 23:3).

While you preach against stealing, do you steal? You that forbid adultery, do you commit adultery? The failure of some Jews to teach themselves is manifested as Paul quotes the Torah that forbids stealing and adultery (Exodus 20:14-15). The Jews have the law, yet they transgress the very law they follow. These series of rhetorical questions—diatribe—in verses 21-23 are denunciatory and might be aimed at confusing the hearer. Paul's goal in using these series of questions, which are common in the letter to the Romans (2:3-4; 3:1-4), is to allow the interlocutor the ability to judge the situation so that he/she can draw his/her own conclusions. You that abhor idols, do you rob temples? This last rhetorical question does not follow

---

[23] Wright, 445.

logically like the accusation of the first two. The conclusion of the last query ought to have been: "Do you worship idols?" Paul is aware that the Jews believe in one God, thus they cannot be accused of idolatry. However, the word Paul used for temple is a pun on Jerusalem; maybe because Jerusalem is a concern for Torah- observant Christians since it is where the temple is located. Paul might be quoting Deuteronomy 7:25 that warned the Israelites not to covet the gifts offered to idols but to destroy the gifts. By Paul quoting from the scriptures, it gives his argument a solid and authoritative backing; hence he establishes his claim that the audience is guilty of the above mentioned crime. For the Jews, taking gifts offered to idols does not contradict the first commandment, since the gifts belong to no one. Probably, Paul is condemning this act because the Jews are selling these stolen valuable artifacts from pagan shrines,[24] instead of burning them as they are commanded by God to do.

Paul might be bringing out an accusation levied on Torah-observant Christians about their attitude toward the sacrifices made to pagan gods, when in actuality they should be a light to their fellow Christians. The act of stealing brings discredit to the Jews and scandal to the Gentile Christians who look upon them as models and guides. Edgar Krentz explains that Israel's temple robbery dishonors God's name because the Israelites were not to "speak disrespectfully

---

[24] Duane Watson, "Paul and Boasting," in Paul in the Greco-Roman World: A Handbook, ed. J. Paul Sampley (Harrisburg, PA: Trinity Press International, 2003), 100.

of the term god, even if it is applied to an idol;"[25] for the respect given
to creation is also directed to the Creator. However, their temple robbery is an act of shame given that they were enriching themselves
with the proceeds from their sales. You that boast in the law, do you
dishonor God by breaking the law? Because of the unfaithfulness of
these Torah-observant Christians, God's name was dishonored. The
Jews were supposed to be a light to attract the Gentiles to God; conversely, their lives betrayed this privilege and brought dishonor and
shame to God. God is the Patron of the Jews, and the Jews as the
clients, were disloyal and unfaithful to their Patron.

Therefore, their disloyalty to the law and robbing of pagan temples brought shame to God's name among the Gentiles. The name of
God is blasphemed among the Gentiles because of you. Here Paul
quotes Isaiah 52:5 which depicts Israel's misfortune and God's compassion toward them.[26] However, in Paul's case, it is an oracle of judgment against Israel for breaking the law they embodied, and turning
the Gentiles away from God. Consequently, the Jews' disobedience
to the Torah not only affected their relationship with the Gentiles,
but also God's honor within this group.

Paul's Emphasis on God's Impartiality

What is Paul's mission or goal in writing this letter? In other
words, what is he looking forward to achieving in a church he had

---

[25] Edgar Krentz, "The Name of God in Dispute: Romans 2:17-29," Currents in Theology and Mission 17, no. 6 (December 1990):436.

[26] Byrne, 101.

not founded? What is the agenda behind his persuasive admonitions and how might this letter change the mind of his hearers? In 1:16-17, Paul expresses that the Gospel is first to the Jews, and then to the Greeks. This view might suggest that there is an anti-Jewish sentiment in this church. The Gentile Christians might not be warm enough in their acceptance of the Jewish Christians who were still struggling to find their bearings in Rome after their expulsion from the Roman Capital in the 40's by Claudius.[27] The Acts of the Apostles recorded that Priscilla and Aquila met Paul in Corinth after they had been expelled from Rome by Claudius (18:1- 3), and at the time Paul was writing this letter, these couples were back in Rome (Rm 16:3-4). This expulsion was probably because of the riot between Jewish Christians and Jews over the status of Christ in the synagogue at Rome. Therefore, Paul's mission might be to bring to the awareness of these Gentiles, that the Jewish Christians are still the root and the Gentile Christians, the branches.[28]

On the other hand, Paul uses this letter to introduce himself to the Torah-observant Christians, and at the same time he explains some issues that had been misinterpreted. One of them might be that Paul was against the Jews that preached that God had abandoned them in favor of the Gentiles.[29] In order to avoid creating an image of the superiority of the Jews, Paul uses a demonstrative rhetorical

---

[27] Witherington III and Hyatt, 16.

[28] Witherington III and Hyatt, 16.

[29] Barry D. Smith, "The Letter to the Romans: The New Testament and Its Context," Crandall University, http://www.abu.nb.ca/courses/ntintro/Rom/htm (accessed October 9, 2010).

and theological argument to express that both Jews and Gentiles are one before an impartial God, and both can work cooperatively to be united in Christ. Inasmuch as the Jews have a law that guides them, the Gentiles also have a natural law that guides them. But these laws do not justify a person, since the Christ-event is superior to these laws. Thus, faith in Jesus Christ justifies one, and baptism, not circumcision provides one access to the God of Abraham. In this way, Paul redefines the meanings of covenant, law, circumcision, and the promise God made to Abraham; all these have new meaning in Jesus Christ.

Paul's intention in this portion of his letter is to promote a good relationship between the Jewish and Gentile Christians. In a bid to achieve this, he demonstrates through the Scriptures, that both Jews and Gentiles have sinned and are in need of God's mercy. Before he does this, Paul diplomatically wins the hearts of these Torah-observant Christians by denouncing the folly of the culture of death that was common among the Gentiles. Finally, Paul points out that the Jews are as guilty as the Gentiles. Not only are the Gentiles adulterous, immoral, and idolatrous, but even the Jews, who are entrusted with the obligation of guiding the Gentiles to the light, have committed these same crimes. Some Jews have not lived up to the expectation of being the embodiment of truth and knowledge, and some Gentiles have not obeyed the natural law inscribed in their hearts. However, both laws—natural and the Torah— participate in God's divine law and both lead Christian Gentiles and Jews to God respectively. This divine law is God's wisdom, and Jesus is the Wisdom of God. Thus, to obey the law is to be connected with the

Wisdom of God. The Gentiles are no less sinners than the Jews, given that all have sinned and have fallen short of the glory of God (3:23). Therefore, the impartial God will judge them through Jesus Christ since neither the Torah nor natural law is sufficient for salvation, for salvation is God's actions through grace.

Paul expects his audience to adhere to his "gospel" since it is in line with the Gospel of Jesus Christ. His writing is very persuasive and convincing, and it calls the Jewish Christians to look inward and see whether what they preached is what they practiced. At the same time, the Gentile Christians would be reprimanded by their consciences for wrong doing. The intention behind this passage is to call the audience to a conversion of hearts; even though Paul uses a diplomatic speech in 15:14-15 to convince the church that he was not writing for conversion reasons. However, this audience will draw their own conclusions from Paul's argument as to whether they are guilty of what Paul confronted them with. Paul's objective, which he diplomatically achieves, is to tell the Roman church of the need to adhere to the Gospel of Jesus Christ since both Christian Jews and Gentiles stand in equal relationship before an impartial God.

SECTION TWO

SHORT REFLECTIONS ON BIBLICAL THEMES

Chapter 9

AN INVITATION TO A SPIRITUAL CLEANSING

"How sweet is the way of Love! True, one may fall, one may not be always faithful, but love quickly consumes whatsoever may displease Jesus."

—St. Thérèse of Lisieux (*Story of a Soul*)

Luke 11:37-41

37While he was speaking, a Pharisee invited him to dine with him; so he went in and took his place at the table. 38The Pharisee was amazed to see that he did not first wash before dinner. 39Then the Lord said to him, "Now you Pharisees clean the outside of the cup and of the dish, but inside you are full of greed and wickedness. 40You fools! Did not the one who made the outside make the inside also? 41So give for alms those things that are within; and see, everything will be clean for you.

Introduction and Short Exegesis

This is the second invitation to dinner from a Pharisee in Luke's account, and each occasion is an avenue for Jesus to admonish the host and the Pharisees (7:36-50). The fact that Jesus does not perform the cleansing ritual astounds the host who is a Pharisee, and who strictly observes the purity ritual. The accounts recorded in Matthew 15:1-9 and Mark 7:1-9 involve the disciple's failure to wash their hands and Jesus' defense of them, but in Luke's account, Jesus is the victim. Rather than defending himself, Jesus attacks the Pharisees for acting hypocritically, and for rejecting God's will for them.

In his speech, Jesus did not express gratitude for the meal rather he shifts emphasis from the surface of the vessels "outside of the cup and the dish," to the interior person, "inside you are filled with plunder and evil." Luke is reminding his readers that the quality of righteousness is expressed in generously sharing one's possessions, practicing justice, and showing love. Interestingly, The New Interpreter's Bible clarifies that Jesus not washing his hands after performing an exorcism, and staying with the crowd in vs. 14-36, scandalizes his host. This commentary also notes that vs. 41 is confusing. What is to be given; is it what is in the cup or what is within a person? Luke might be telling his reader that a person's actions should reflect his/her inner purity. Luke finally recommends inward over outward purity. This reflection is an invitation to attend to our spiritual clean up, over outward purity.

An Invitation to a Spiritual Cleansing

A story was told of a strange, shabby-looking man who hurriedly entered the church on a Sunday to worship with the faithful. He was late and the pews appeared full. He could have been accommodated in some of the pews, but no one even made room him. He had not taken a bath for some days and he resembled a homeless man. This reminded me of what St. James 2:1-7 said about preferential treatment. We accord more respect to rich people with fine clothes and look down on poor people, dressed in shabby clothes. It seemed like the shabby man was not welcome in this community of worshippers. They looked down on him because his outer garments were unclean.

In this gospel passage, Jesus taught that while outer cleanliness is important, inner cleansing is more crucial—a compassionate heart, a generous welcome and hospitable spirit. Yes, Jesus was invited to the Pharisee's house as an act of kindness, but he encountered a host who started out in an inhospitable way because he neglected the pre-scribed washing before a meal. The host, it appeared, did not even offer him the water needed for the washing. We were not told why Jesus did not perform the ritual before eating. Maybe he had just washed before his visit; if his hands were clean, they didn't need to be washed again. Perhaps he was starving and couldn't wait to eat since he had been teaching the crowd and casting out demons. Most likely, Jesus might have seen an opportunity to teach, and teach he did!

One would have expected the host to keep himself busy in serv-ing and caring for the guests. However, because of self-righteousness, he seemed more hung up on the thought of the washing ritual which was the most insignificant part of the occasion, and he missed out on the salvation Jesus brought to his household. Jesus was appalled to find out that he completely lacked an understanding of what true spirituality and worship of God is. Thus, Jesus was quick to teach him that almsgiving, kindness, charity in thoughts, words and actions cleanse our inner life. These virtues are opposite to greed, envy, self-ishness, bitterness and an unwelcoming spirit that come from within us. When our inner life is clean, it reflects our true identity as God's children, and it gives real meaning to the outward ritualistic cleanliness.

The man I spoke of earlier smiled at his unwelcoming friends, walked quietly to the front pew where there were a few empty seats, and sat down. After the Mass, there was fund raising for the church's building. The strange-looking man pledged to give half of his wealth to the building of the church. This amount was more than enough to complete the building that had lingered for over ten years. He told them his story which was that he had slipped and had fallen, which knocked him unconscious for two whole days. When he finally regained consciousness, it was Sunday and he didn't want to miss the Mass. Taking a shower was the last thing on his mind, and he staggered as he ran to church to give thanks to God for saving his life. I would bet that those who had judged him to be a poor, dangerous, homeless man, unworthy of their company, learned a little lesson on charity and hospitality that day.

Jesus is inviting us to do some spiritual cleansing. I do not think that any of us would be comfortable in an unkempt room. Thus, a clean heart is the foundation of a clean life. This involves compassion, kindness, love, generosity, hospitality, and forgiveness. Who knows, we might feed or feast with Jesus through people we come in contact with. In that way, we experience the salvation Jesus brings to our life daily. Cleaning up for hygiene's sake is very necessary, but cleaning the soul has even more significance because it reflects on the outside. The shabby man's inward purity was manifested by his generous offering and thankful heart. However, those who judged him before hearing his story were skeptical and cynical. They lacked charity. Therefore, the identity of an authentic and real Christian is manifested by acts of charity. We are called to be more compassionate and kind to ourselves and to one another.

Chapter 10

REMAIN IN MY LOVE

Charity gave me the key to my vocation...I understood that love comprises all vocations, that love is everything, that it embraces all times and all places because it is eternal! At last I have found my vocation. My vocation is LOVE."

—St. Thérèse of Lisieux (*Story of a Soul*)

John 15:9-12

Jesus said to his disciples: "As the Father loves me, so I love you. Remain in my love. If you keep my commandments, you will remain in my love, just as I have kept my Father's commandments and remain in his love. I have told you this so that my joy might be in you and your joy might be complete. This is my commandment: love one another as I love you."

Introduction and Short Exegesis

In this section are parts of Jesus' discourses to his disciples before his death, which runs from chapters 13-17:26. The passage follows the vine and branch metaphor, where Jesus depicted himself as the vine and the disciples, as the branches. Jesus knew his death was at hand (Jn. 12:7) and thus he needed to initiate his followers into his oikos (household) through the washing of their feet. He completed this initiation ceremony with this farewell discourse.

In African culture, just as it was in the culture of Jesus, a person who is nearing death is believed to be wiser and closer to the ancestors, and thereby having the ability to see beyond what is purely physical. This farewell discourse, which is only found in John's gospel, was meant to strengthen the disciples, who in this case were Johannine community, expelled from the synagogues for believing in Jesus' divinity (Perkins 1990, 945). The expulsion was implied in the story of the man born blind. His parents were afraid to defend him for fear of being expelled from the synagogue (Jn. 9:22-23). Pheme Perkins believes that the crises faced by this community, after this expulsion, might have led to the anti- Semitic nature of John's gospel, and possibly the geographical relocation of the Johannine community from Palestine to Ephesus (Perkins, 946).

The persecution faced by the Johannine community, made an intimate relationship with Jesus necessary so that they would develop their identity around him. The commandment to love would have helped them remain firm on the Vine, and to bear fruit that would last (Jn. 15:16). Perkins also believes that there might be division among this community caused by different meanings attached to the traditions they had inherited (Perkins 946), which could be another reason for the admonition to love one another, as well as to remain in Jesus' love. The Johannine community seemed to be faithful in following Jesus, even when some disciples were leaving Jesus because of his difficult teachings (Jn. 6:60-69).

According to St. Thomas Aquinas, this passage makes three points: "To remain in Jesus is to remain in his love; to remain in his love is to keep his commandments; and this commandment is to love" (Aquinas, 104). The text begins with: As the Father loves me. For Aquinas, "as" indicates equality of nature or likeness of grace and love (Aquinas, 104). The implication of this statement is that the source of love is God, and the disciples are loved by Jesus with the same manner of love that the Father has for Jesus. Ultimately, Jesus extends the mutual love between him and his Father to the disciples and commands them to abide in his love. However, this is not without a condition, which is to keep Jesus' commandments.

Francis Moloney explains that this abiding is shown in a way of life determined by the commandments of Jesus, just as he kept his Father's commandments (Jn. 4:34) and remained in his love (Moloney 1998, 421). Aquinas demonstrates that the disciples cannot keep the commandments without grace, since God influences and helps us to do his will (Aquinas, 105). Basically, Jesus does not demand from the disciples what he did not model; his obedience mirrors a life-style expected from his disciples.

Verse 11 explains that joy is the end result of keeping Jesus' commandment. This joy is the disciples' consolation, and it is contrary to the sorrow they would experience with his departure. In other words, the assurance of joy would be experienced by the branches (disciples) when they abide in the Vine that produces abundant love. The summary of this discourse was expressed in verse 12, "This is my commandment: love one another as I love you." In Matthew and Luke, (Mt. 5:44, Lk. 6:27) the command was to love one's enemies, but in John, the command to love could be interpreted as love among the Johannine community or among the followers of Jesus. However, it is the love that all the disciples of Jesus are to be identified by in the world.

The kind of love used in this section is agapē and it appeared seven times. For Aquinas, this love is charity which is the beginning and end of every virtue. He explains that everything has its source in charity, and everything is directed to charity as its end (Aquinas, 107). Consequently, love must be selfless, unconditional, and efficacious as Christ's love is; thus, the phrase "…as I love you."

Remain in my Love: A Wedding between a Muslim and a Christian

God is the source of divine love. Thus, when a man and a woman decide to tie the knot, they are participating in this divine love. A marriage that is founded on God's love is not intended to be a passing celebration, but a state of being that lasts for life. The clarion call of Jesus is clear: "Love one another as I love you;" "Remain in my love;" Keep my commandment;" and "Your joy will be complete."

The mutual love between spouses must entail obedience to God's will, mutual submission and respect for each other, as well as a love that bears the weaknesses and failings of one another. Champlin and Jarret explain that to remain in marriage requires the capacity to share physical and emotional spaces, even when it is tempting to withdraw, as well as the courage to practice mutual listening and communication even when this is uncomfortable (Champlin & Jarret 2012, 83).

In his book, "Love Beyond Reason: Moving God's Love from Your Head to Your Heart," John Ortberg explains that God's love for us is beyond reason; meaning that God creates us not out of necessity, or need, or because He is bored and lonely, but rather because He loves us. We are gifted with the capacity to love, and we naturally seek to love and be loved. I believe that the love flowing from God is what brought Ahmed and Libby (not their real names) together. Otherwise it could be nearly impossible for a Christian to marry a Muslim or vice versa.

I came from a country where some radical Muslims and some Christians do not see eye to eye. Churches and mosques are set ablaze in the name of religious bigotry, and people are killed, kidnapped or maimed in many of the conflicts. Bombs are detonated and hundreds of people killed. God did not create us to hate each other, but rather to love. The union between Libby and Ahmed can teach us that genuine love exists. Their union exemplifies that love transcends religion, race, and cultural differences. It is a lesson to us that we can live together peacefully in love without strife. St. Thomas Aquinas calls this love charity. Charity is the beginning and end of every virtue. With charity there will be no jealousy, hatred, envy, wars, conflicts, terrorist attacks, or discords. Sometimes our competitive spirit get the best of us, and we try to prove that our religion is better. Ahmed and Libby would not have been willing to be joined together in marriage if they were competing on who is smarter, better, more professional, or more talented. Such selfish behavior in a marriage or in society will prove to be unproductive and even destructive. But to remain in love, is to avoid every unhealthy competitive spirit.

Ahmed, I don't know when you first met Libby, or the circumstances that led to it, but I am sure that so much has happened since then. You have seen the positive as well as the negative side of each other. Your parents, relatives, and friends may have given their opinion why the two of you should not be together. Obviously, you have learned to love and appreciate each other in spite of all the odds. When we were having a chat concerning their relationship, I asked Ahmed and Libby their experiences of loving each other. They explained that it was challenging, even for them to believe that it would work. The experience of their parents and family members is yet another story. But what kept them together was that they learned to remain in love, to be proud of each other, to build each other up, to treat each other with reverence, and to praise the unique gifts of each other. Thus, for a couple to remain in love involves bearing with each other selflessly, sharing emotional, physical, and communal spaces even when it is challenging to do so. And to be aware that there is no perfect marriage!

An anecdote was told of a man who went out seeking a perfect woman to marry, but he never got married because there was no perfect woman. However, he almost had the chance to marry a gracious lady he had met, but she was also looking for a perfect mate and he was not perfect for her. There is no marriage that happens in sixty minutes, or sixty days, or even sixty weeks; perhaps though sixty years can qualify. Thus, as you wed today, know that marriage is not the dress, the ceremony, the honeymoon, the sex, or the change of name. Rather it is the mutual commitment to the love you profess to each other and to God. Let your union be a model to our war-ridden world. Let the language of "me" and "my" give way to "us," "ours," and "God's" so that your love may grow into maturity.

When we are young, our first word of choice of word is "me," "my," or "mine." Young children think everything is theirs. I see this in my little nephew who thinks that everything belongs to him. Give him a gift and ask for it later, and you will be surprised when he flat-out refuses to give it back. But when we grow older, we realize that there are other people in the world, and we learn to say "ours." I want to believe that your language has also changed from "my" and "me" to "ours" and "us." This attitude of sharing and inclusivity will bring joy and fulfillment to your marital union.

Jesus speaks of this joy in our reading. Couples who remain in God's love find joy and fulfillment. The joy promised by Jesus is a complete and abundant joy. Sometimes the joy that comes with love might not be pleasurable, because it involves sacrifice especially when the couple are discovering the flaws in each other. However, to remain in love and in marriage, the couple needs to learn how to bear with each other in love. Love never gives up. It hangs on. It holds on. You can count on it. Love gives and serves the loved one without expecting a return, just as God loves and serves us unconditionally. Love listens and pays attention to the beloved. Listening to one another is very important in a relationship.

Think for a moment of the comic strip scene depicting a couple at the breakfast table. The husband is reading a newspaper as the wife is sharing her frustration with him. The wife complains that the husband is not listening to her and the husband shouts, "Do you want me to repeat every word that you have just said?" What the wife needs at that time is the presence and attention of the husband, and not the replaying of her words. Therefore, give maximum attention to each other and it will increase your mutual love and joy.

As you come before the people of God to profess your vows, know that you are participating in His divine. Let your union be an example to teach every religion that we are created for one purpose and that purpose is love. St. Augustine explains that "Love slays what we have been so that we may be what we were not." We ask God to give you the grace, the patience, and the compassionate heart to remain in God's love so that your joy may be complete.

Chapter 11

GOD SHOWS NO PARTIALITY

"I feel that when I am charitable, it is Jesus alone who acts in me; the more I am united to Him, the more I love."
—St. Thérèse of Lisieux (*Story of a Soul*)

Acts 10:34-38, 44-48 (NRSV)

34Then Peter began to speak to them: "I truly understand that God shows no partiality, 35but in every nation anyone who fears him and does what is right is acceptable to him. 36You know the message he sent to the people of Israel, preaching peace by Jesus Christ—he is Lord of all. 37That message spread throughout Judea, beginning in Galilee after the baptism that John announced: 38how God anointed Jesus of Nazareth with the Holy Spirit and with power; how he went about doing good and healing all who were oppressed by the devil, for God was with him. 44While Peter was still speaking, the Holy Spirit fell upon all who heard the word. 45The circumcised believers who had come with Peter were astounded that the gift of the Holy Spirit had been poured out even on the Gentiles, 46for they heard them speaking in tongues and extolling God. Then Peter said, 47"Can anyone withhold the water for baptizing these people who have received the Holy Spirit just as we have?" 48So he ordered them to be baptized in the name of Jesus Christ. Then they invited him to stay for several days.

God Shows no Partiality

From experience, I know how partiality abounds in my country, Nigeria. Nigeria is divided into two geographical zones, the north which is predominantly Muslim, and the south which is mostly Christians. Before one gets admission into a university or employment in either of these zones, one has to indicate their religion and tribe. The reason for this stereotyping is to favor first the Muslims or the Christians depending on which zone one is searching for the school or job. This is the highest form of favoritism I have witnessed. Thus, it is your religious affiliation/ tribe, and sometimes your "purse," not necessarily your qualifications that would aid a northerner or southerner in getting admission to the opposite geographical zone. I am sure Ahmed that you might also have the experience of partiality in Northern Nigeria.

But whatever kind of partiality we experience, we read from the passage above that God shows no partiality but in every nation, anyone who fears Him and does what is right is acceptable. It does not matter to which religion you belong. The scene of our reading is the house of a Roman Centurion, a Gentile. He experienced conversion and Peter was sent to minister to him. Ordinarily, as a Torah-observant Christian, Peter would not have gone to the house of a Centurion. But in his dream, a vision was given to him not to call anything created by God unclean. From Peter's dream, he realized that God loves everyone—Greek, Gentile, or Jew, Christian or Muslim. Similarly, Peter is expected to love without partiality if he claims to be a follower of God. The evidence of God's impartiality was the outpouring of the Holy Spirit on all who were listening to Peter, and they were all baptized.

We have gathered to baptize Ibrahim and Rebekah, two precious gifts from God to Ahmed and Libby. You are privileged to participate in co-creating with God. The expectation is that you will bring them up in the fear of God. With God's help, they will grow up to be virtuous by observing the loving union between you (Ahmed and Libby) and through your guidance. The baptism they will receive will grace them into becoming new creatures and adopted children of God. They will be renewed in body and spirit, Original Sin forgiven; and they will become members of the Church, and temples of the Holy Spirit. I know Ahmed that Muslims do not baptize, however they believe that God is the dispenser of grace. As I was preparing this reflection, I read through some chapters of the Koran. I found that each chapter of the Surah starts with this acclamation "In the name of Allah, the most gracious and the dispenser of grace." It is this grace that the Spirit of Allah will bestow on your children—Ibrahim and Rebekah, and the grace of baptism will sanctify, heal, and purify them.

The same Surah explains that it was Allah who sent down the Torah of Moses and the Gospel of Jesus as guides for humankind (Surah 3:3- 4). The message of Jesus as explained by Peter is the message of peace, impartial love, and doing what is right. I believe that these past five years have been life-giving and challenging for you Ahmed and Libby, in your marital life. You might have seen the best and worst of each other and sometimes you exclaimed, "This is not what I bargained for!" You might have swam in an ocean of doubt and fear as you contemplated whether or not your choice of spouse was truly the one made for you, or if it was a mistake. Why? Because when you (Libby) need his listening ears, he tells you that he is tired from work. When you request him to join you in visiting your family for Thanksgiving, he tells you he would rather be with his family. When you (Ahmed) plead with her to make a cup of soup for you, she tells you to do it yourself. When each baby arrived, you struggled with what name to give each child—a Christian or a Muslim name, and in which religion to raise them. What about who gets to change the diapers in the middle of the night? (I am just making all these things up) With all these frustrations to deal with, you still remember your marital vows and the need to be available to each other.

All these challenges and more could have split your union, but you stood firm in your love for each other. The Catholic Bishops in the U.S. capture the importance of interreligious marriage when they write: "Families arising from an interreligious marriage give witness to the universality of God's love which overcomes all division. When family members respect one another's different religious beliefs and practices, they testify to our deeper unity as a human family called to live in peace with one another" (USCCB, "Follow the Way of Love"). Your marital union witnesses to this universality of God's love which is impartial in nature. It is this impartial love that I pray will continue to grace your union. Not like the partiality that fills our world today, especially in a country like mine where your religion gets you into a university or a lucrative job. May the grace of God sustain your loving union and assist you in bringing Ibrahim and Rebekah up in God's impartial love.

Chapter 12

A CALL TO SING ALLELUIA EVEN IN THE MIDST OF TRIALS: A REFLECTION ON A SHROVE TUESDAY

"To offer oneself as a victim to Divine Love is not to offer oneself to sweetness or to consolation; but to every anguish and every bitterness. For Love lives only by sacrifice; and the more a soul wills to be surrendered to Love, the more must she be surrendered to suffering."

—St. Thérèse of Lisieux (*Story of a Soul*)

If there is only one word that could summarize our sacred liturgy, that word is alleluia. Alleluia is a Hebrew word which literally means "Praise God." It is one of the Hebrew words with hosanna and amen, that were not translated into Latin or English. Alleluia is a joyful word! It is an Easter word! Today we have gathered to sing alleluia. But from tomorrow until Easter vigil, alleluia, will be "buried." Why? Because we are entering a holy season! A period the Church has designated for communal fasting, praying, and almsgiving. A season that reminds us of our salvation history, and what Christ went through in order to reconcile us with God! A time when we silently contemplate on why God sacrificed his Son in order to redeem us! A season of penance and sober reflection! A time we reflect on God's immeasurable love for humanity! It is a season that calls us to carry our crosses daily and follow Christ.

As Christians, carrying our crosses is inevitable since suffering is part of life. Although human suffering is not something to be desired, it is sometimes connected to the Paschal mystery experience and thus becomes a blessing in disguised. However, the hardest element of suffering is the feeling of abandonment or rejection of the Divine that suffering normally evokes in us. This was the experience of Jesus on the cross when he cried out to God, "My God, my God, why have you forsaken me?" When such moments come and we are not able to sing alleluia, we should take solace in knowing that Christ had the same feeling. St. Paul puts it well that the "message of the cross is foolishness to those who are perishing, but to us who are being saved, it is the power of God" (1 Cor. 1:18).

Certainly, it is hard to sing alleluia when that cross seems heavy, just as it was hard for the Israelites to sing Zion's song in a foreign land. Have you ever encountered a hopeless situation where it was difficult for you to sing alleluia or even to pray? In such moments you may wonder whether God still exists. I certainly have. Consequently, Psalm 42:9 comes in handy: "I say to God my Rock, "Why have you forgotten me?" My own experience of feeling the absence of God was when I visited my older brother (Fr. Vincent) at Baptist Hospital in Little Rock, after his automobile accident in January 2007. He was in the Intensive Care Unit with a spinal cord injury which had rendered him paralyzed, and he was undergoing surgery. He could not move his hands, his feet, or any part of his body. On that sad day, I was not able to pray. I asked God so many questions and I cried day and nights for the two weeks I was with him. My two

Sisters, (Sr. Kathleen Howard, and later Sr. Eileen Ann O'Keeffe), supported me in my pain.

But what kept my hope alive was my brother's meeting with a psychologist who was doing a routine interview. This interview is conducted with patients after severe trauma in order to assess how every patient is doing in the midst of their experiences. She asked him so many questions but three stood out for me: "Do you have nightmares?" My brother answered no. "Do you regret your accident?" My brother answered no. "Are you depressed?" My brother answered no. She was surprised at his answers and paused. Then my brother raised his head, smiled at her, and asked, "Do you really want to know the truth?" The psychologist changed her posture and was ready to hear the truth since she thought that my brother had not been honest. My brother said, "The truth is this, nothing will ever take away my joy and peace of mind. These two— joy and peace of mind—will be the last to die in me since their source or foundation was not from material things but from God." That day became a memorable one for me, because before then, I had felt so down and depressed seeing his condition. His positive attitude toward suffering transformed me. It became an Aha moment!

It is important to know that in suffering and in pain we stand alone before God waiting to be filled. We accept what we cannot change, and accept the fact that we are not God. We trust that God is in charge. Jesus accepted his pain because of his love for humanity, and his love in doing his Father's will. My brother Vincent, accepted his situation as something he could not change. His joy was not in his lost arms and legs at the time of the accident, (he has regained his mobility) but in the consolation that God is in charge. As Christians, we should be aware that our suffering is in communion with Christ's suffering. This awareness gives great consolation and awakens in us the temporality of human suffering. It gives us energy to focus not on the cross, but rather on the salvation of humankind that was achieved through it.

The Lenten season reminds us of our daily suffering, our daily deaths, and our daily crosses. We are parting from alleluia because it is a song of victory over death, and we hope in the goodness of God to remain victorious over sin. This does not mean we will cease from praising God. But it is silencing the joyful word—alleluia—in order to participate in the suffering of Christ. May our Lenten season be grace-filled! And may we be blessed with the grace to trust in God in the midst of suffering, and the willingness to sing alleluia not only at Easter, but ultimately on the day we will meet the Lord face-to-face. That day we will praise God without ceasing, by singing: Alleluia! Alleluia!! Alleluia!!!

Chapter 13

LEADERS ARE SERVANTS

"I crave no other Throne nor other Crown but Thee, O my Beloved."

— St. Thérèse of Lisieux (*Story of a Soul*)

Mt. 23:8-12

8But you are not to be called rabbi, for you have one teacher, and you are all brethren. 9And call no one your father on earth, for you have one Father, Who is in heaven. 10Nor are you to be called masters, for you have one Master, the Messiah. 11The greatest among you will be your servant. 12All who exalt themselves will be humbled, and all who humble themselves will be exalted.

Reflection

Have you ever worked under a boss and you always work with fear and tension? Think of the people you are afraid of either because of their autocratic power, their place in the family, or their influence as head of schools, hospitals, companies, government institutions, business partners, spouses, etc. Sometimes you feel so inferior in their presence because you think you cannot measure up to them. Before I joined religious life, I worked in a bank as a cashier. Our bank manager was extremely tough and scary. The senior employees, including the accountant and deputy manager, were terrified of her;

how much more the junior staff members such as myself. Whenever she went on a business trip or took a vacation, the atmosphere of the banking hall was peaceful and jovial. We all worked with a cheerful spirit, so unlike the tension and strain we all felt from dealing with her bossy attitude, and constant fault finding.

In the passage above, Jesus explains the model of leadership that is required of us. "The greatest among you will be your servant." This is hard to imagine! How can the greatest among us serve others, rather than exercise their authority and expect those under them to do the service? In our world today, the greatest among us make their position felt. Recognition, prestige, and praise matter a lot. Sometimes we get carried away by these external honors. Other times, we use our position of trust to exploit others and devalue them. However, Jesus explains that leadership is service. It flows from the love we have for God and for one another. Leadership does not impose heavy burdens on others. Moreover, it is both strong and gentle. It is similar to a well-known saying about maintaining boundaries in a professional setting: be friendly but not a friend. Humility is at the core of servant-leadership.

There is a story about Abraham Lincoln's humility, and the bid to devalue him by his opponents. On the first day after being elected as the president of the United States of America, Abraham Lincoln was to give his first presidential speech. As he entered, one of the rich aristocrats among the Senators got up and said: "You should not forget that your father used to make shoes for my family." The whole Senate laughed thinking that they had made a fool of him. With humility and wit, President Lincoln looked him straight in the eye and replied: "Sir, I know that my father used to make shoes for you and many others here. He was an unmatched cobbler. He was a creator. His shoes were not just shoes, he poured his whole soul into making them. I want to ask you, have you any complaints? If you have, I can make another pair of shoes for you because I am a good cobbler. But I know that no one has ever complained about my father's shoes. I am proud of my father." The whole Senate was quiet.[1]

President Lincoln's acceptance of his humble beginnings brought shame to those who were out to devalue him. He could have been swallowed in self-pity, but he accepted the challenge in humility. Humility is not timidity, unassertiveness, or low self-regard It is however lack of pride and meekness of heart. Jesus' great emphasis on humility made him to condemn the hypocrisy of the Pharisees and our own hypocrisy too.

Throughout the four gospels, instances abound where Jesus admonished us to be humble. In Luke 9:46-48; 22:24-30, Jesus asked the disciples to be child-like by placing a child before them, when they were struggling for position in the reign of Christ and asking who will be greatest in heaven. In Luke 14:8-11, Jesus told the parable of a wedding feast that resulted in the guests grabbing the best seats of honor, and he concluded with the call to humility. After narrating the parable of the two men who went to pray in the temple, (Luke 18:10-14) Jesus praised the one who humbly acknowledged that he was a sinner and concluded with the same call "for all who exalt themselves will be humbled." Jesus did not only call us to be humble,

---

[1] https://www.movemequotes.com/abraham-lincoln-son-shoemaker/

he became a model for us by washing the feet of his disciples and instructed them to do likewise.

We are challenged to be servants to one another. I recall that one of the titles of a Pope is "Servant of the servants of God." Being a Pope makes him a servant of the Church. St Augustine has this to say during the sermon of the anniversary of his ordination: "For you I am a Bishop; with you, I am a Christian." He continued: "I am terrified by what I am to you, but comfortable by what I am with you. The first is a title; the other is a name of grace. The first means danger, and the other salvation." The implication is that the title, although an honor, could cause our downfall if we are carried away by its glory. But when our position is used in the service of others, then it will bear fruit. Our community will become a home of equals, where the talents of everyone are appreciated; where each person is a brother or a sister; and God is our Father and Mother in heaven; and Jesus Christ, our Friend and Brother. It will not be a hierarchical gathering where tension and fear hinder growth like my former bank manager, or where we devalue one another like the Senators to Abraham Lincoln, but rather a fellowship of equal members who work together to bring about the reign of God.

Chapter 14

PATIENCE IS VERY REWARDING

"Seeing that the eternal reward is so disproportionate to the small sacrifices of this life, I longed to love Jesus, to love Him ardently, to give him a thousand proofs of tenderness while yet I could do so."
—St. Thérèse of Lisieux (*Story of a Soul*)

James 5:7-10 (NRSV)

7Be patient, therefore, beloved, until the coming of the Lord. The farmer waits for the precious crop from the earth, being patient with it until it receives the early and the late rains. 8You also must be patient. Strengthen your hearts, for the coming of the Lord is near. 9Beloved, do not grumble against one another, so that you may not be judged. See, the Judge is standing at the doors! 10As an example of suffering and patience, beloved, take the prophets who spoke in the name of the Lord.

Reflection

Patience is an important virtue in the life of every Christian. Patiently waiting for the coming of Christ is compared by St. James to the waiting of the farmers for the seasonal rain. However, as the farmers wait for the early rains, they have other jobs, such as plowing the field and removing the weeds and stones. In the same way,

Christians are to prepare the soil of their souls by doing righteous work. At least the farmers have a clue when to expect the rain, but Christians do not have any idea of the Parousia. Thus, they have to bear all suffering patiently as did the prophets.

The natural ability to remain calm and not become agitated or annoyed in difficult situations or in dealing with a "difficult personality" is rare. Pains and trials push our buttons to respond with impatience. However, some temperaments are calmer and therefore these personalities are more patient than others. Personally, having more patience is one of the areas that I continue to work on. Whenever I have lost patience in frustrating situations, I always come to the realization that having a little more patience would have been better. Actually, it is like a thorn in my flesh which I have begged God to take away from me, but he always answers, "My grace is enough for you." I am learning the art of patience. Although patience is a virtue, one can cultivate it through conscientiously practicing it.

One summer, my younger sister Gloria and her two year old son Joe, were flying to Arkansas to visit our older brother. Their flight from Detroit, Michigan was landing in Chicago and they would board another flight from Chicago to Memphis. During the one hour layover, she took Joe into the restroom to change his diaper. Afterwards she went to throw it away in the garbage right outside the door. Thinking that Joe was right beside her, she turned around, but did not see him. Where could he be? He had been right by her side. She entered the bathroom again to check whether he was there, but he wasn't. Gloria called out his name, but there was no answer. If there was someone in that bathroom, she could have concluded that Joe had been kidnapped. She didn't know what to do. She was totally confused and the only thing she could hear herself saying was "Jesus do not abandon us." By the side of the restroom was an elevator. She did not know that Joe had pressed the button and when the door opened walked right into it. Thank God he was not able to press any other button that would have taken him either up or down. After a few seconds that seemed like an eternity, the elevator opened and he emerged from it smiling. The effect of his disappearance confused her so much so that she had not even noticed the elevator until Joe came out from it. However, her patience in staying at the scene paid off.

In the reading above, St. James urges his audience to be patient until the coming of the Lord. This may have been an exhortation that was needed by his audience because of the injustice they faced at the hands of the rich (James 5:4-6) and because of their own personal trials. As James urged his audience to be patient, he also prescribed how: instead of complaining, they should bear their hardships gracefully, imitating the prophets who had endured their ordeals as they proclaimed God's word. At this time, there was an expectation that Christ was coming back soon, so the early Christians had to be continually reminded to wait patiently just like a farmer waits patiently for the rains.

We are also called to be patient in whatever situation we find ourselves. As the saying goes: "Good things come to those who believe, better things come to those who are patient, and the best things come to those who don't give up." Impatience is manifested in grumbling and judging which seem like signs of hopelessness. Have you ever gone shopping when things are on sale and you waited and waited in long lines? Or perhaps you have been caught up in a long traffic jam when you have an appointment or interview for a job and you are running late? What did that feel like? Certainly these can be trying and irritating situations, and can push our "red buttons."

It is said that patience is not so much the ability to wait, but how we act while we are waiting. Our patience is tried in the little things and trials of life and sometimes we get frustrated and upset. But the good news is that perseverance and patience are always rewarding. At least the farmers know when to expect the early rains, but we do not have any idea when to expect Jesus or when to expect trials. We have to be sober so as not to lose focus because of impatience. If my sister had left the scene of her son's disappearance, who knows what could have happened. However patient endurance and God's divine intervention solved the mystery of my nephew's disappearance.

Another saying goes that, "God makes a promise; faith believes it; hope anticipates it; but patience quietly awaits it." We are called to wait patiently as the farmer does for the promises of God to be revealed. If we have faith in Christ; trust him in and out of season; our reward will be great! We ask God for the grace to live faithfully and patiently as we await the coming of our Lord Jesus Christ.

Chapter 15

SEEKING THE LORD AT THE WELL OF OUR SOULS

"Ah! Since the day Love penetrates me and surrounds me;
His Merciful Love each moment renews and purifies me,
leaving in my heart no trace of sin."

—St. Thérèse of Lisieux (*Story of a Soul*)

John 4:3-42

3 He left Judea and started back to Galilee. 4 But he had
to go through Samaria. 5 So he came to a Samaritan city
called Sychar, near the plot of ground that Jacob had given to
his son Joseph. 6 Jacob's well was there, and Jesus, tired out
by his journey, was sitting by the well. It was about noon.

7 A Samaritan woman came to draw water, and Jesus said
to her, "Give me a drink." 8 (His disciples had gone to the city
to buy food.) 9 The Samaritan woman said to him, "How is it
that you, a Jew, ask a drink of me, a woman of Samaria?"
(Jews do not share things in common with Samaritans.) 10
Jesus answered her, "If you knew the gift of God, and who it
is that is saying to you, 'Give me a drink,' you would have
asked him, and he would have given you living water." 11 The
woman said to him, "Sir, you have no bucket, and the well is
deep. Where do you get that living water? 12 Are you greater
than our ancestor Jacob, who gave us the well, and with his
sons and his flocks drank from it?" 13 Jesus said to her, "Everyone who drinks of this water will be thirsty again, 14 but
those who drink of the water that I will give them will never

be thirsty. The water that I will give will become in them a spring of water gushing up to eternal life." 15 The woman said to him, "Sir, give me this water, so that I may never be thirsty or have to keep coming here to draw water."

16 Jesus said to her, "Go, call your husband, and come back." 17 The woman answered him, "I have no husband." Jesus said to her, "You are right in saying, 'I have no husband'; 18 for you have had five husbands, and the one you have now is not your husband. What you have said is true!" 19 The woman said to him, "Sir, I see that you are a prophet. 20 Our ancestors worshiped on this mountain, but you say that the place where people must worship is in Jerusalem." 21 Jesus said to her, "Woman, believe me, the hour is coming when you will worship the Father neither on this mountain nor in Jerusalem. 22 You worship what you do not know; we worship what we know, for salvation is from the Jews. 23 But the hour is coming, and is now here, when the true worshipers will worship the Father in spirit and truth, for the Father seeks such as these to worship him. 24 God is spirit, and those who worship him must worship in spirit and truth." 25 The woman said to him, "I know that Messiah is coming" (who is called Christ). "When he comes, he will proclaim all things to us." 26 Jesus said to her, "I am he, the one who is speaking to you."

27 Just then his disciples came. They were astonished that he was speaking with a woman, but no one said, "What do you want?" or, "Why are you speaking with her?" 28 Then the woman left her water jar and went back to the city. She said to the people, 29 "Come and see a man who told me everything I have ever done! He cannot be the Messiah, can he?" 30 They left the city and were on their way to him.

31 Meanwhile the disciples were urging him, "Rabbi, eat something." 32 But he said to them, "I have food to eat that you do not know about." 33 So the disciples said to one another, "Surely no one has brought him something to eat?" 34 Jesus said to them, "My food is to do the will of him who sent me and to complete his work. 35 Do you not say, 'Four months more, then comes the harvest'? But I tell you, look around you, and see how the fields are ripe for harvesting. 36 The reaper is already receiving wages and is gathering fruit for eternal life, so that sower and reaper may rejoice together. 37 For here the saying holds true, 'One sows and another reaps.' 38 I sent you to reap that for which you did not labor. Others have labored, and you have entered into their labor." 39 Many Samaritans from that city believed in him because of the woman's testimony, "He told me everything I have ever done.

40 So when the Samaritans came to him, they asked him to stay with them; and he stayed there two days. 41 And many more believed because of his word. 42 They said to the woman, "It is no longer because of what you said that we believe, for we have heard for ourselves, and we know that this is truly the Savior of the world."

Reflection

In December 2004 in Kenya, a baby hippopotamus survived the tsunami waves on Kenyan Coast despite losing its mother. The hippo was so traumatized that it formed a strong bond with a giant male century-old tortoise named Mzee, in an animal facility in Mombasa. They swam, ate, and slept together and if any one approached the tortoise, the hippo became aggressive, as if protecting its biological mother. These are animals, yet they know the importance of setting apart their differences in order to comfort each other. Jesus sets apart the social and religious differences in order to bring to faith the Samaritan woman and her people.

Jesus was in the Samaritan city of Sychar where he was taught not to go, and much less talk with people from that town. But Jesus was exhausted and thirsty. He sat at Jacob's Well, probably praying that somehow he might quench his thirst, but he had nothing to drink from. Here comes a woman! "Oh thank God!" he probably thought to himself. At least his needs would be met. Gail O'Day on "John" in the Women's Bible Commentary explains that the nameless woman is an outsider and a foreigner, thus it is a scandal for Jesus to speak with her, and worse still to ask her for water.

The Samaritan woman had a lonely life. The men in her life have either divorced her or have died. We were not told whether she has children. She went to fetch water at a time when she was sure to not meet anyone, but she ended up meeting Jesus who knew everything about her. Dianne Bergant and Richard Fragomeni in Preaching the New Lectionary noted that the woman's character is questionable: she is alone at the well at an ungodly hour; she has married five husbands when the Law of Moses frowned on more than three marriages; and she engages in a conversation with a strange man. Jesus was the first to break the social and religious boundaries between the Jews and the Samaritans. Firstly, he made his way through the Samaritan town; and secondly he prompted a conversation with a woman whom he would not talk with under normal circumstances.

When Jesus asked for water, the woman was not comfortable with the request. She was surprised that Jesus was asking for water from a woman he was taught to despise. Jesus did not condemn her, but rather he engaged her in a dialogue that brought her to faith. Subsequently, Jesus revealed his identity to her. At the end of their conversation, the lonely woman was filled with joy. Her real thirst was quenched and she left her jar behind; probably also her old way of life. Transformation took place at the well and the woman became a disciple of Jesus. Because the Samaritan woman was open to the transformation Jesus was offering, the barrier was broken, the enmity vanished, and the indifferences healed, just like the story of the young hippo and Mzee that found consolation in the company of each other.

Where is the well where we can meet Jesus? This well is within us. Jesus is the one who quenches our thirty souls. Jesus is thirsting for our friendship, our love, and our faith. He is at the well of our soul, beckoning us to come and quench our thirst. Let us respond to his loving invitation.

Chapter 16

THE VOICE OF ACCEPTANCE!

"O my God, Most Blessed Trinity, I desire to love Thee and to make Thee loved"

—St. Thérèse of Lisieux (*Story of a Soul*)

I am a Samaritan. My life has always been that of disappointment, rejection, suffering, and loneliness, because all the men that came into my life have either died, divorced me, or become separated from me. I even became a laughing stock among my people. Neither my family members, nor my fellow women wanted to be associated with me. This rejection turned me into a nameless woman. In all these painful experiences, I still believed in the God of our ancestors, and hoped that the promised Messiah would come and reconcile us to our kinsmen— the Jews—who had become our enemies.

On that fateful day, I was going to draw water at the well of Jacob. I would normally go late to avoid meeting anyone on the way. I was alone because none of the other women wanted to keep company with me. Seated at the well was a Jew, and I was wondering what he would be doing in the territory of his people's enemies at this ungodly hour. I wanted to go back home, but I bravely continued with my task, reminding myself that the place belonged to my people, so I had the right to be there. Actually if anyone should leave, it should be him. On approaching the well, I was astonished to hear him ask me for a drink! Did I hear him correctly? A Jewish man talking with and requesting a drink from a woman in public; a woman who happened to be from a tribe he was taught to despise? This was not possible and it startled me! I just wanted to be sure that I heard him right. I asked him, "Do you really want a drink from me, a Samaritan woman?"

He changed the topic and started talking about a living water that quenches thirst forever, of which he is the source. This man is strange, I thought. He has no bucket to draw with and the well is deep. Where was he going to get that living water from? Is he greater than Jacob our ancestor who gave us this well and drank from it himself? The more he talked, the more unusual he sounded. Then I begged him to give me that extraordinary water of his, so that I would not waste my time coming to the well.

Then came the awkward moment when he asked me to go and call my husband. That is a topic I would not want anyone to talk about. Why was this strange man asking for my husband? I had to answer sincerely, after all he is a stranger and a Jew. And sure enough he knew I was telling the truth. Was he a prophet to have known that I had lived with five men? He even taught me how to worship God in truth and in spirit. But I was aware that the promised Messiah would come and teach us everything. Could this stranger be him? I wondered to myself. Yes, I am the Messiah, he responded.

I was overwhelmed with joy. His voice was gentle and sweet to my ear. He did not condemn or devalue me as my community members would do, but he looked into my eyes with compassionate love. He accepted me and made me feel comfortable in his presence. I felt like my dignity was restored. I found my voice again. I am alive! The loneliness in my heart was filled with this awesome experience. He was no longer a stranger but my friend, my master, and my companion. He quenched my thirst and I left my jar. I left my old way of life. I was transformed! I have to tell everyone who cares to listen to me so that they may experience the overflowing joy that this experience has brought into my life. I felt accepted, valued, and loved. Thus, I became one of the voices of acceptance. I became a witness.

Are you lonely and isolated like me? Has your sin made you a stranger to Jesus? Are you thirsting for living water that will quench the thirst of your brokenness and heal you? Turn to Jesus now! When you come face-to-face with Jesus, your dejection, suffering, loneliness, misery, and isolation will become history. Experiencing Jesus gives way to acceptance, love, hope, faith, and cheerfulness.

Chapter 17

THE VOICE OF WRATH:
AMOS AND THE CORRUPT LEADERS

"I will work for your Love alone. My sole aim being to give You pleasure, to console your Sacred Heart, and to save souls who will love You forever."

—St. Thérèse of Lisieux (*Story of a Soul*)

Background Information

There is no true prophet who is devoid either of suffering or of death. For Jeremiah it was: "Let us cut him off from the land of the living, so that his name will no longer be remembered" (Jer 11:19). Jesus Christ, the greatest prophet, experienced the same fate and even declared that a prophet is without honor in his home land (Mk 6:4). The writer of James explains how some prophets were stoned to death, others killed by sword, while others were persecuted and tormented (Jas 11:32, 37). Although Amos was not killed, he was rejected for challenging the status quo and exposing the exploitation of the poor by the rich. Because he announced the fall of the reigning dynasty of the northern kingdom of Israel, he was denounced by the chief priest Amaziah and advised to leave the kingdom (7:10-13).

Amos did not start out as a prophet, but was a sheep herder and a sycamore fig farmer (7:14). He was from the southern kingdom of Judah and God appointed him to go and prophesy to the northern kingdom of Israel, particularly the cities of Samaria and Bethel (7:13) during the reign of Jeroboam II. He was one of the Minor Prophets who spoke against the disparity between the rich and poor, the social corruption in the land, and the oppression of the poor. His major theme was social justice and God's divine judgement on the rich who trampled upon the poor.

Amos condemned the rich who sold the poor into slavery when they are unable to pay their debts. Some poor people used their land or their cloak as collateral, and these were taken by the rich when the debt could not be paid (2:6-8; 8:5-6). Amos denounced: the rich merchants who trampled on the heads of the poor by using false scales in their business (8:5); the landlords who bought the poor for a pair of sandals and rendered them landless (2:6); the priests who enjoyed the rich offerings and abundant sacrifices at the expense of the poor (4:4-5); and the elders who perverted justice at the gate in favor of the rich because of bribery (5:10-11, 14-15; 8:4-6). The poor suffered at the gate at the hands of the elders who were supposed to defend them. All these for Amos were religiosity without righteousness. For him, justice and righteousness come with refraining from oppressing the poor.

Isaiah captured the picture well when he expressed that princes (leaders) loved bribes and ran after gifts; they did not defend the fatherless and the widows, rather they were friends to the thieves (Is 1:23). Micah as well condemned the unjust leaders who perverted justice and coveted the fields of the poor and the needy without redress (Mic 2:2; 3:1-3). As a result of bribes, the guilty were acquitted and the innocents were deprived of their rights (Is 5:18-28).

What did the leaders do with this wealth? They were drinking the choicest wine like the "cows of Bashan" at the expense of the poor (4:1). Amos later advised them to hate evil and seek good, to establish justice at the gate, and God might be gracious to them (5:14-15). For Amos, sacrifice and ceremonial rituals have no value without justice and righteous deeds: "I hate your feasts and your solemn assemblies. Your burnt offerings and your cereal offerings I will not accept. Take away from me the noise of your songs… but let justice roll down like waters, and righteousness like an ever-flowing stream" (5:21-24). He concluded that anyone who seeks the Lord will live (5:4, 27) but failure to repent, will result in God allowing them to go off into exile.

The Voice of Wrath!

The voice was very loud and clear, "Condemn him, kill him, let us accuse and condemn him to a shameful death, so that our land will be peaceful again for our gain." But why will you kill me? What offense have I committed? I am not even a prophet. I was only called by God from my work as a herdsman and a dresser of Sycamore trees to prophesy against the mistreatment of the poor, since their cry has reached heaven.

The Lord has condemned you! Corrupt leaders and the rich who sold the poor into slavery in foreign land and caused some to become refugees in their own lands. The Lord has condemned the rich merchants who trampled on the heads of the poor by using false scales in their business, and selling substandard goods to the poor. The

Lord has frowned on you priests who enjoyed the rich offerings and abundant sacrifices at the expense of the poor without condemning the atrocities of the rich. And you elders, who perverted justice at the gate in favor of the rich because of bribery, the Lord is watching you. The rich who used the poor as sex slaves to satisfy their sexual urges, and the leaders who deprive the laborers of their rightful wages, the Lord is furious at your ugly deeds. All these sins will not go unpunished because the Lord has denounced them.

For your transgressions corrupt political leaders, who took bribes and neglected the cries of the poor, who delighted in killing your children because they condemned your iniquities; see, your sentence has been written! God shall visit you with his wrath because you accepted bribes at the expense of the poor. All you evil government officials will be swallowed up by the graves you have dug for the innocent. You will plant and never harvest. You will eat and drink and never be satisfied. The selfishness of the leaders and the shameless attitude with which you loot the wealth of the nation is evidenced by your lifestyle, and your bank accounts. You "cows of Bashan," you drink choicest wine at the expense of the poor. The wrath of the Lord is upon you! All the corrupt wealth you have accumulated shall be stored in a leaking coffer. Thus, when you need the money to satisfy your selfish desires, you will hold an empty coffer.

For you corrupt leaders, listen! The Lord has something in store for you. You who used two different measures in your dealings with the poor and the rich. Where is justice? Where is your human conscience? Prejudice has so blinded you that you no more consider the consequences of your actions. You have rendered the land barren.

You have caused the land to quake. You have torn it open and made the poor suffer. Of what use are the seas when the food in them is poisoned, the water unsafe for drinking? How will the poor survive when their only means of survival (food, air, and water) has been polluted from industrial waste? The poor can no longer enjoy basic necessities of life such as good drinking water, good health care, good roads, good housing, etc.

The Lord has commanded that his children be treated with respect, not like slaves. Their rights are to be respected: the right to a healthy living and safe environment, the right to enjoy the unpolluted air God has blessed them with, the right to have food daily on the table, the right to express themselves without the fear of being harmed, the right to education in a safe environment, the right to dignity, justice, and the right to worship God without the fear of being persecuted and killed.

Thus says the Lord, when you become selfless, when you allow justice to overflow like a river in the land, when you remember the poor of the land and alleviate their conditions, when you fulfill what is written in the constitution, then God will turn his face toward you and look kindly upon you. When you repair the cracks in the land, treat people like human beings created in God's image, and use the same measure for both the rich and poor; when you use the resources of the land equitably for the betterment of everyone; when you administer justice and condemn bribery; when you pay the laborers their fair wage and listen to the cry of the poor; then the Lord will relieve the wrath he has placed upon you.

But rejoice, you land, the poor, the homeless, the unemployed, the abused, the rejected, as well as those inflicted with different kinds of ill health. For the Lord who executes judgment has rescued his people. No longer shall you be plucked up from your land. For the Lord of vengeance has exalted the horns of the righteous. The Lord has visited his people. Let the nations be glad for the Lord has done great things. Let the sea and all that fills it rejoice. Let the barren land shout for joy. Let the mountains exclaim in triumph. For the right hand of the Lord has delivered his people from the slavery of corrupt leaders. Praise be to the God of our ancestors!

Chapter 18

DO YOU WANT TO BE HEALED?

"But on whom shall our poor heart lavish its love? Who shall be found that is great enough to be the recipient of its treasures? It is Jesus! He alone can give us back infinitely more than we shall ever give to him."

— St. Thérèse of Lisieux
(Letter to her cousin, Marie Guerin)

John 5:1-16 (NRSV)

1After this, there was a festival of the Jews, and Jesus went up to Jerusalem. 2Now in Jerusalem by the Sheep Gate there is a pool, called in Hebrew Beth-zatha, which has five porticoes. 3In these lay many invalids—blind, lame, and paralyzed. 5One man was there who had been ill for thirty- eight years. 6When Jesus saw him lying there and knew that he had been there a long time, he said to him, "Do you want to be made well?" 7The sick man answered him, "Sir, I have no one to put me into the pool when the water is stirred up; and while I am making my way, someone else steps down ahead of me." 8Jesus said to him, "Stand up, take your mat and walk." 9At once the man was made well, and he took up his mat and began to walk.

Now that day was a Sabbath. 10So the Jews said to the man who had been cured, "It is the Sabbath; it is not lawful for you to carry your mat." 11But he answered them, "The man who made me well said to me, 'Take up your mat and walk.'" 12They asked him, "Who is the man who said to you, 'Take it up and walk'?" 13Now the man who had been healed did not know who it was, for Jesus had disappeared in the crowd that was there. 14Later Jesus found him in the temple and said to him, "See, you have been made well! Do not sin anymore, so that nothing worse happens to you." 15The man went away and told the Jews that it was Jesus who had made him well. 16Therefore the Jews started persecuting Jesus, because he was doing such things on the Sabbath.

Introduction and Short Exegesis

Reflecting on this reading one observes that this man was not the only one at the pool. Why did Jesus single him out for healing? The scripture recorded that the paralyzed man had been there for thirty-eight years. Were there no relatives to help him into the stirred water all those years? What is the significance of taking up the mat? Did he need the mat since he had been healed? In other miracles, the sick person had always been the one to approach Jesus for healing. Why did Jesus initiate this healing?

Francis Moloney on "The Gospel of John" in Sacra Pagina Series noted that Jesus was going for a feast in the Temple, but this feast was not mentioned. Jesus' question ("Do you want to be well?") to the paralytic man, who had been at the pool for thirty-eight years, was unlike him. Nevertheless, the question enabled conversation. Teresa Okure, writing on "John" in The International Bible Commentary explained that the paralytic man was right to say that he had no one to help him into the water when the angel stirred it, since it is only

Jesus who could help him and forgive his sins. This is in line with the admonition of Jesus to him later, "Look you are well now; do not sin anymore." The argument of Okure is that sin can paralyze the soul and drain one from enjoying life in God. The paralytic man's obedience to Jesus' command "Rise, take up your mat, and walk" showed that he trusted and had faith in Jesus even without knowing him. Okure observed that this obedience showed his willingness to take up responsibility for his life, instead of the mat carrying him for thirty-eight years. Okure explained that the word "rise" was also used by Jesus in the raising of Jairus' daughter. Thus, the paralytic man was as good as dead without Jesus.

When the Jews confronted the paralytic man because of breaking the law of the Sabbath, he blamed the unknown healer for his action. It was obvious that the Jews were not interested in the healing, but they were interested in the one who commanded someone to break the Sabbath law. Moreover, by revealing to the authorities the identity of the healer, the man was simply giving credit to Jesus and witnessing to his power to heal.

Do you want to be healed?

If your legs were paralyzed for thirty-eight years and then through God's intervention you were healed, how would that change your life? While travelling to Nigeria during the summer of 2018, I experienced numbness in my legs because I had sat for eight hours without stretching them, and my blood circulation was poor. I was not able to stand for a few minutes, and even that seemed like an eternity. This man had been paralyzed for thirty-eight years! Can you imagine that for thirty-eight years this man had been seated on the mat? There were no wheelchairs in those days to help him move from one place to another, unless he had relatives to carry him and take him where he wanted to go. But he did not have relatives to assist him to go into the water when an angel stirred it.

Jesus was attending an unnamed feast at the Temple in Jerusalem. On approaching Bethzath (meaning House of Mercy), he realized that the paralytic man had been there for a long time. He asked him whether he wanted to be healed. This is unlike the miracles Jesus had performed. Usually the sick person was the one to initiate the healing, but here Jesus was moved to recognize the predicament of this man. The man actually did not know who was asking him such an obvious question. Of course he needed healing, that was why he had been at the pool for thirty-eight years.

In answering the question, the man called to Jesus' attention that he had no one to help him into the pool when the water was stirred up. This was admitting that he could not help himself. Yet with great patience, he had been at the pool of mercy waiting for the Lord of mercy to appear. Out of compassion, Jesus told him to rise up, to take his mat, and to walk. The man was under the providential care of God's mercy and goodness. What a joyful moment for the man to feel his legs moving. No wonder he wanted everyone (including the Jews who asked him why he was breaking the law of the Sabbath) to know that it was Jesus who had healed him.

My older brother had an automobile accident in 2007. His spinal cord was affected and his legs were partially paralyzed. He was bedridden for six months and was getting some physiotherapy. Seven months after the accident, the feelings began returning to his legs. A year after the injury he was able to move his legs, and this was the happiest day of his life. He called me and told me about the miracle. I was overwhelmed with joy because I knew what he had gone through. My brother's joy was similar to the joy of the paralytic man.

What is paralyzing our souls? Do we recognize our need for healing? Where and from what do we need Jesus to heal us? There is a saying that the solution to a problem begins with the ability to recognize its existence. Jesus is asking us, "Do you want to be healed?" Are you paralyzed from saying yes to this question? It is only the sick that seeks a physician. Are you aware of what ails you? It is time to reflect on our paralysis. Reflect on: when we could have shown love and we chose not to love; when we could have forgiven and we chose to bear grudges; when we could have been generous with our time, and we chose to be selfish. What is paralyzing our ability to love, to forgive, and to be kind? Jesus is asking us again: "Do we want to be healed?" If our answer is "Yes," then we will rejoice like the paralytic man and my older brother who both experienced the healing power of God. And thus, we will become the healing presence of God in our chaotic and war-stricken world.

Chapter 19

GRATITUDE IS THE BEST ATTITUDE

"I long to console You for the ingratitude of the wicked! I thank You, O my God, for all the graces You have bestowed on me"

—St. Thérèse of Lisieux (*Story of a Soul*)

Luke 17:11-19 (NRSV)

11On the way to Jerusalem Jesus was going through the region between Samaria and Galilee. 12As he entered a village, ten lepers approached him. Keeping their distance, 13they called out, saying, "Jesus, Master, have mercy on us!" 14When he saw them, he said to them, "Go and show yourselves to the priests." And as they went, they were made clean. 15Then one of them, when he saw that he was healed, turned back, praising God with a loud voice. 16He prostrated himself at Jesus' feet and thanked him. And he was a Samaritan. 17Then Jesus asked, "Were not ten made clean? But the other nine, where are they? 18Was none of them found to return and give praise to God except this foreigner?" 19Then he said to him, "Get up and go on your way; your faith has made you well."

Introduction and Short Exegesis

Luke T. Johnson writing on "Luke" in Sacra Pagina Series explained that these ten lepers were at the border between Samaria and

Galilee where Jesus was passing, which was evidence that they were living outside of camp as directed in Numbers 5:2-3. They were supposed to be shouting to warn people from coming close to them, but here they shouted for mercy and even recognized Jesus as "Master." The command, "Go and show yourselves to the priest" is to fulfill the legal requirement, since the priest had to confirm the cure before they could be allowed to return to normal life in their communities (Lev 14:1-4). Of the ten lepers, only the Samaritan leper came back worshipping and giving thanks, which are signs of humility and faith.

The significance of specifying the Samaritan's identity is similar to the story of the Good Samaritan who showed generous love, in contrast to the Jews who neglected the needs of a fellow Jew who had been attacked by robbers. Karris Robert in The New Jerome Biblical Commentary mentioned that the Samaritan leper was the only one who fully understood what had happened, and his returning to Jesus suggested conversion. This Samaritan leper glorified God for what Jesus—God's servant—had done. However, the other nine went to announce the good news (probably to their communities) after being confirmed clean by the priest, and never came back to thank Jesus. Thus, this story's theme is the importance of being grateful, and Jesus' response is a sign that it is normal to feel hurt by ingratitude.

However, in our ungrateful attitude, God still loves us and shows us compassion. Sometimes we take things for granted. Because the sun should always rise in the morning and set in the evening, we do not ponder on it and thank God for his creation. Because we have food on the table and we are able to feed ourselves, to take a good warm bath, and dress ourselves up, we do not recognize that our hands and feet are gifts. Although we are called to be grateful, our ingratitude does not stop God from loving us, just as it did not stop Jesus from healing the lepers. But the issue is that the other nine received only physical healing, while the Samaritan leper received an additional spiritual healing. Thus, it is left for us to choose only a physical healing or both.

Gratitude is the Best Attitude

A story was told of a man who was in a dream and went to heaven. At the gate, St. Peter welcomed him, showed him around, as he explained what each angel was doing. Some angels were extremely busy at a particular post, and St. Peter explained that it is the "Receiving Section," where all the petitions to God said in prayer were received. The second post was equally as busy as the first one with many angels working very hard. St. Peter also explained that this is the "Packaging and Delivery Section," where the graces and blessings the people asked for were processed and delivered to the persons who asked for them. They came to the third post where there was only one angel who was not busy. St. Peter clarified that here is the "Acknowledgment Section." But the man asked: "How is it that there is no work going on here?" St. Peter sighed and replied: "After people receive the blessings that they ask for, very few come back to give thanks."

We read from the passage above how ten lepers, who were living outside of their homes, received healing, but only one returned to give thanks. Having an unclean sickness alienated and separated these men from their communities, family members, and friends (Lev 13:45-46). In ancient Israel, community mattered a lot. Because these lepers shared the same fate and shame of being lepers, and thus suffering rejection, they found meaning in forming a family among themselves. Although under normal circumstances, a Jew and a Samaritan would never be part of one household because they do not see eye to eye, these lepers came together as a community and shouted unitedly: "Jesus, Master, have mercy on us." They must have expected Jesus to say a word or touch them just as Jesus had done in Luke 5:12-15, but Jesus instructed them to go and show themselves to the priest. Probably, Jesus was testing their faith, since it was only after being healed that one was supposed to see a priest. Perhaps also they were grumbling on their way and they did not notice changes on their limbs, feet, and body. However, Jesus' instruction was a sign that they were healed, and going to the priest was to confirm this healing just as the book of Leviticus 14:1-4 instructed.

Only the Samaritan man paid attention to his healing, and he did not see the need to visit a priest. Rather he returned to Jesus to thank him for restoring him to his community and for removing the shame he had faced for many years. Jesus was amazed that only a Samaritan had returned to show gratitude. "Where are the other nine?" Jesus asked. Most likely they were Jews who knew God and the Torah. Were they not moved to praise God who had made their cure possible?

We often experience God's compassion, yet sometimes we do not show appreciation. This story is no longer the story of the ten lepers, but our story. Every day we wake up in the morning, fit and strong to help ourselves. We have the sun to brighten our day. We have air to breathe, a roof over our heads, food on our tables, and prayers answered. But is gratitude our attitude? Remember there are millions who lack these basic needs, and there are millions who are handicapped and cannot use their hands and feet.

I was visiting some patients in the hospital one day, and I found myself beside the bed of a patient that was totally bedridden. He was unable to take a shower by himself, brush his teeth, or feed himself. He said to me after our visit, "We do not know the value of what we have until we lose it. You cannot imagine how I have missed the joy of taking a shower by myself, brushing my teeth, or feeding myself." His words brought tears to my eyes and really challenged me to be mindful of the miracles in my daily life. It taught me a great lesson, and reminded me that it does not cost a dime to say "Thank you God," or even to thank people who have helped me. Gratitude rather helps me to grow in the awareness that everything I have is a gift from God, and to develop the attitude of saying "thank you."

Even though God does not need our thanks to show us mercy, we still need to show appreciation. May we reflect on the graciousness of God in our daily lives, and thank God. Let us also develop the attitude of expressing our gratefulness so that we can keep the "idle angel" in our story very busy as well. Gratitude is certainly the best attitude!

Chapter 20

COMPASSION: THE ONLY WORD THE DEAF CAN HEAR

"Charity must not remain shut up in the depths of the heart, for no one lights a candle and puts it under a bushel, but upon a candlestick, that it may shine to all in the house. (Matthew 5:15). It seems to me that this candle represents the Charity which ought to enlighten and make joyful, not only those who are dearest to me, but to all around me."

—St. Thérèse of Lisieux (*Story of a Soul*)

Mk 6:30-34

30The apostles gathered around Jesus and told him all that they had done and taught. 31He said to them, "Come away to a deserted place all by yourselves and rest a while." For many were coming and going, and they had no leisure even to eat. 32And they went away in the boat to a deserted place by themselves. 33Now many saw them going and recognized them, and they hurried there on foot from all the towns and arrived ahead of them. 34As he went ashore, he saw a great crowd; and he had compassion for them, because they were like sheep without a shepherd; and he began to teach them many things.

Introduction and a Short Exegesis

In Preaching the New Lectionary, Dianne Bergant and Richard Fragomeni stated clearly that it was in this pericope that the term "apostle" was first used for the twelve to signify their mission of being sent to share in the ministry of Jesus. The deserted place Jesus invited them to, is where Jesus normally went to pray. The return of the disciples to a deserted place is a return to a more reflective life after participating in the ministry of Jesus. Jesus was sensitive to the disciples' needs, and his compassionate heart moved him to attend to their spiritual and physical needs. John Donahue and Daniel Harrington in the "Gospel of Mark," in Sacra Pagina Series, are of the view that "rest" may also have an eschatological meaning. The letter to the Hebrews (4:9-11) stated how God promised rest from toils and persecution to those who sought him. Jesus also assures rest to all who come to him with weariness of heart and who are carrying heavy loads (Mt 11:28-29).

On the other hand, the crowd must have tasted Jesus' superabundant love, and because of that they hastened even on foot to be with him. They must have also experienced the good works of God through the Apostles when they were sent out to evangelize (Mk 6:7-13). Bergant and Fragomeni explained that Jesus' compassion for the crowd was a profound inner emotion which has a Messianic significance and depicted Jesus' deep love for those who sought him. It was the same tradition in Mk 1:42, where Jesus had compassion on the leper and restored his health. Perhaps the people were searching for guidance, miracles, direction, or a dependable leader, and not necessarily a search motivated by spiritual experience. Yet Jesus taught them, fed them, and became their shepherd, because he noticed that they were like sheep without a shepherd.

In reflecting on this passage, these questions guided me: What is the meaning of this rest? Why was the crowd looking for Jesus? Why did Jesus fail to dismiss the crowd since he and the disciples were resting? How did Jesus notice their need for a shepherd? With many voices claiming to have the solution to every problem, how do I discern the voice of a Good Shepherd among them? If I am to be a shepherd, how compassionate will I be in walking my sheep along both rosy and stormy paths?

Compassion: The Only Word the Deaf Can Hear

Imagine how beautiful our universe would be if compassion touches it! Compassion is not sympathy or empathy; it is moving beyond empathy to action. Compassion is the empathetic consciousness of another's distress and the desire to alleviate it. It is different from love because it can be given to a stranger without a deep feeling of affection or love. It is exemplified in a story told about Nelson Mandela. In the 1950's, Mandela saw a white woman standing next to her broken car in Johannesburg.

He approached her and offered to help. After fiddling around with the engine, he fixed the car. Thankful for his help, she offered to pay him sixpence. "Oh no, that's not necessary," Mandela said, "I am only too happy to help." "But why else would you, a black man, have done that if you did not want money?" she asked quizzically. "Because you were stranded by the side of the road," Mandela replied.[1]

---

[1] https://world.time.com/2013/12/06/5-great-stories-about-nelson-mandelas- humility-kindness-and-courage/

Compassion has the combination of love, concern, consideration, empathy, care, and kindness. It is one of the attributes of God, (Ex. 34:6-7 and Ps. 86:15) "The LORD the LORD, merciful and compassionate/gracious, slow to anger, abounding in steadfast love and faithfulness.

Today our world is facing chaos. When one picks up the daily newspaper to read, turns on the radio or television, or browses through the internet or social media, the news headlines are filled with violence, riots, racism, bomb blasts, shootings, stabbings, kidnappings, terrorist attacks, depressions, religious wars, economic crises, abuse of all kinds, immigration problems, sickness and viruses of different kinds, etc. What if each person on earth practiced even a little compassion, what kind of world would we have? Compassion does not only benefits the receiver, but also the giver. It is not about how much is given, but doing the ordinary little act of kindness helps to make this world a better place. Mother Theresa of Calcutta explained it clearly that we should learn to do the ordinary things of life with an extraordinary love.

There is a story of a student who was not able to pay his tuition, because he was an orphan. So he wrote a letter addressing the envelope to God without a destination, but including a return address. He wrote: "God, I am not sure whether you exist and where you live, but if you do exist, please send to me 30 dollars for my school fees." When the postmaster saw the letter addressed to God without a destination, he opened it and read it. He said to himself, "Even though I do not believe that there is a God, I will send the sum of $30.00 to this student since it is for his tuition. It is equally a small amount that

I could afford." When the student received the money, he confessed: "Truly there is a God. He not only replied to my letter, but he also showed me compassion." What is our response to the need we see? Not everything is about money or charity to the poor, what about our brothers and sisters in our communities or neighborhoods who need a shoulder to lean on? Do we provide ours or do we sometimes pass by like the two men in the story of the Good Samaritan?

Jesus is challenging us with his compassionate heart. He was sensitive to both the needs of his disciples for rest, and the needs of the crowds who were helpless and without a shepherd. Jesus told the disciples to come and rest awhile. What kind of rest is this? I believe it is not the eschatological rest, but a moment to be with one's self in a reflective mood. How often do we listen to Jesus' invitation to join him in a deserted and quiet place? This passage resonates with me as well because sometimes I overburden myself, and I may not even hear the invitation of Jesus to come and rest awhile. I like getting things done in a timely manner, and sometimes do not make enough time for myself. Consequently, I get burnout at times. It was Socrates who said that an unexamined life is not worth living. Out of compassion, Jesus is inviting me and all of us to rest in his heart that is filled with love.

This deserted and lonely place Jesus is inviting us to, is within us; the deepest part of our soul where we are sometimes afraid to visit. Do we create time to pray and to reflect on how faithful God has been to us? Do we also make time to be with families, friends, and community members without being distracted with cell phones, text messages, emails, Facebook, Instagram, LinkedIn, Snapchat, Twitter,

WhatsApp messages, television programs, and every kind of social media connections? Jesus is calling us into a deeper relationship with him by inviting us to rest in his compassionate love. If we are aware that to those who need rest, God is their rest; to those who need a shepherd, God is their guide; to those who are helpless, God is their source of hope, then we will reach out and embrace God's free gift— compassionate love.

If we listen attentively, we will experience the love of Jesus that is immeasurable. We have two ears and one mouth for a reason, thus we should listen more and talk less. When we have received and experienced

Jesus' compassion, we can courageously and consciously be the hands and feet of Jesus to show compassion to all people. The atheist postmaster was used by the God he did not believe in to show compassion. Without knowing it, he became the hand of God's compassionate love to the poor boy. Mandela was a hand that God used to show compassion to a person who devalued him.

It is obvious that compassion could exist without any relationship. It is an action ridden word and it is selfless. That is why a deaf person who does not hear, can hear and understand compassion, and the blind can see it.

Chapter 21

WHO DO PEOPLE SAY THAT YOU ARE?

"I understood that the Church has a heart and this heart is burning with love; that it is love alone which makes the members work."

—St. Thérèse of Lisieux (*Story of a Soul*)

Matthew 16:13-19

13Now when Jesus came into the district of Caesarea Philippi, he asked his disciples, "Who do people say that the Son of Man is?" 14And they said, "Some say John the Baptist, but others Elijah, and still others Jeremiah or one of the prophets." 15He said to them, "But who do you say that I am?" 16Simon Peter answered, "You are the Messiah, the Son of the living God." 17And Jesus answered him, "Blessed are you, Simon son of Jonah! For flesh and blood has not revealed this to you, but my Father in heaven. 18And I tell you, you are Peter, and on this rock I will build my church, and the gates of Hades will not prevail against it. 19I will give you the keys of the kingdom of heaven, and whatever you bind on earth will be bound in heaven, and whatever you loose on earth will be loosed in heaven."

Introduction and short Exegesis

As I reflect on this Scriptural passage, these questions were ringing in my mind: What do I believe about this text? Why would Jesus wish to know what his people and even his apostles thought about him? Were the disciples also confused about Jesus? Why would the people compare Jesus to John the Baptist, Elijah, Jeremiah or one of the prophets, and why were these figures who were mentioned important? Why did Matthew include Jeremiah, even though his source Mark did not? Who is Jesus to me? If I had to ask the same question to my friends, what kind of answer would I get? In other words, who do people say that I am?

Benedict Viviano explains in "The Gospel According to Matthew" in The New Jerome Biblical Commentary that the "Son of Man" was a messianic apocalyptic title that Jesus used for himself. Viviano continues that Peter was correct in identifying Jesus as the Messiah, and the Son of the living God as opposed to the people who speculated that Jesus might be John the Baptist, Elijah, Jeremiah, or one of the prophets. However, the identification of Jesus by Peter depicts him as the anointed One and the long awaited Messiah who would save Israel. The Sacra Pagina Series, "The Gospel of Matthew," by Daniel Harrington, also clarifies that the phrase "Son of the living God" illuminates any false impressions related to the messiahship of Jesus since he was to be a suffering Messiah. Harrington also noted that John the Baptist had been beheaded and thus, Jesus was suspected of being his reincarnation. Elijah was taken up to heaven (2 Kg 2:11) and the Israelites were expecting his return (Mal 4:5-6, Mt 17:10-13). Matthew added Jeremiah who was not originally in Mark's narration, probably because in his own experiences of suffering and rejection, he announced figuratively the rejection and suffering of

Are?

Jesus. Matthew also mentioned Jeremiah's prophesies in chapters 2:17 and 27:9.

Peter however, received not only a blessing in a beatitude form, "Blessed are you Simon," but also a change of name from Simon to Peter. He happened to be the only disciple who was blessed by Jesus. Peter was also entrusted with a leadership role since it was not "flesh and blood" that revealed Jesus' identity to him. Harrington explains that the word church (ekklēsia) was mentioned by Matthew twice (18:17), probably to distinguish their new church community from the synagogue. Finally, the keys to the kingdom of God given to Peter, indicate the kingdom as being a place to enter (Mt 7:21).

Who Do People Say That You Are?

Imagine Jesus walking up to you right now, as you read this book, and ask: "Who do you say that the Son of Man is?" What will be your response? What is your understanding of Jesus and how does it influence your relationship with him? What if we turn the question around and ask our friends who they think we are. What kind of response will we get?

In this passage Jesus throws a challenging question to the disciples. He wants to discover his identity among his people, and to learn what the disciples think about him. He starts with the Socratic method of teaching: "Who do you say that the Son of Man is?" The Son of Man was the name Jesus had applied to himself, and was used by Daniel in 7:13. Mathew's author likely wishes to identify with the earthly Jesus. He was aware that the crowd and his people did not truly understand who he was. But he was not sure about his closest disciples who had witnessed his teachings and many miracles; yet from time to time they still revealed their weak faith in Jesus.

When the disciples respond to the question, Jesus challenges them with another question: "But who do you say that I am?" Wow! I wondered how the reaction of the disciples was at this simple but challenging question. Some of the disciples might have thought, is this not Jesus, son of Mary and Joseph, whom we hope will deliver us from Roman colonialism? Jesus wanted to be sure that the disciples were not following him so that they could sit at his right and left hand in his "earthly kingdom," when he would conquer the Roman government and win freedom for Israel. But rather, that they were following him because he is the suffering Messiah and that his kingdom is not of this world.

Simon's response, through the insight from God, saved the situation. Thus, he was renamed Peter—Rock. A name probably signifying his leadership role among the disciples and the future ministry which Jesus would entrust to his care after his resurrection: "Simon, son of Jonah, do you love me? ..... "Tend my Sheep" (Jn. 21:15-17). Jesus is called the Christ or the Messiah; names that mean "the Anointed One" which are applied to kings. This name depicts Jesus as a Man for humanity. He lived this identity by dying on the cross, thus saving the entire human race as a suffering Messiah. How do the names we were given reflect on who we are and how we live our daily lives?

In African culture, names are given according to the situation in the family, what God has done for the family, and according to the season when one is born. This name gives one an identity and a sense of belonging. You can tell the gender of a child by his/her first name. When I was born, I was named Adaku and was baptized with the name Helen. Adaku means "wealthy daughter" and Helen means "light." One name suggests that I am the wealth of the family, and the other name carries the expectation to be the shining light. Isn't it a contradiction that I took the vow of poverty as a Catholic religious/nun? How will wealth come to the family through a vow of poverty? I am sure that by following the itinerant Master and Friend—Jesus Christ, who has no place to lay his head, I can strive to be a light and a treasure to, not only my family members, but also to all humanity.

What names were you given and how do they reflect in your daily living? We are called Christians—followers of Christ, light of the world and salt of the earth. Do these attributes reflect the way we witness Jesus? Jesus was called the Messiah and he lived out his Messianic role by sacrificing his life for the sake of humanity. Simon was called the Rock, and he was the first to help the disciples stand on their feet after the Pentecost event. In what ways can our lives and identities reflect Jesus whom we are following? Who does Jesus say that you are? Who do people around you say that you are?

Chapter 22

RECOGNIZING THE VOICE OF THE GOOD SHEPHERD

"Since You O my God has so loved me as to give me Your only Son to be my Savior and my Spouse, the infinite treasures of His merits are mine. To You I offer them with joy, beseeching You to see me only as in the Face of Jesus and in His Heart burning with Love."

—St. Thérèse of Lisieux (*Story of a Soul*)

John 10:11-18 (NRSV)

11"I am the good shepherd. The good shepherd lays down his life for the sheep. 12The hired hand, who is not the shepherd and does not own the sheep, sees the wolf coming and leaves the sheep and runs away— and the wolf snatches them and scatters them. 13The hired hand runs away because a hired hand does not care for the sheep. 14I am the good shepherd. I know my own and my own know me, 15just as the Father knows me and I know the Father. And I lay down my life for the sheep. 16I have other sheep that do not belong to this fold. I must bring them also, and they will listen to my voice. So there will be one flock, one shepherd. 17For this reason the Father loves me, because I lay down my life in order to take it up again. 18No one takes it from me, but I lay it down of my own accord. I have power to lay it down, and I have power to take it up again. I have received this command from my Father."

Introduction and Exegesis

As I reflected on this passage, these questions resonated within me: What does this metaphor of sheep and shepherd mean? When Christ uses the word "good shepherd" it means that there are also bad shepherds. What makes one a bad shepherd? What does it mean to compare humans to sheep? Jesus is a good shepherd, am I a good sheep? Do I recognize and listen to his voice when he calls me? Am I better than the hirelings? Do I experience Jesus' care as the shepherd of my soul? If not, what blocks me from this experience?

Dianne Bergant and Richard Fragomeni's Preaching the New Lectionary explain that the phrase "I am" suggests another form of Divine revelation found in Exodus 3:14. For them, being "good" means being noble, effective, and gracious rather than skilled, since Jesus is committed to the wellbeing of his sheep, in contrast to the shepherds who allowed the sheep to be eaten by wolves. Samuel Ngewa writing on "John," in the African Bible Commentary noted two actions of Jesus for the sheep: Jesus is willing to lay down his life for the sheep and also willing to bring back other sheep that do not yet belong to the fold, in order to have one shepherd and one flock. Ngewa also compares the intimate relationship between Jesus and the Father as equivalent to the love Jesus has for his sheep. Bergant and Fragomeni clarify that this deep and caring relationship is contrary to the shepherding of a hired laborer, who takes care of the sheep out of selfish motives, after all they are not his. They note that the metaphor of sheep may sound offensive to contemporary society, but for the people of Jesus' time, the relationship between sheep and shepherd was a deep one since the sheep knew their owner and recognized his voice. For Bergant and Fragomeni, Jesus' shepherding is unique because he guides and saves the sheep without a weapon or the use of force, and provides for their spiritual and material needs. He also has power to lay down his life and to take it up, signifying his power over life and death. He calls each by name and they listen to his voice.

Recognizing the Voice of the Good Shepherd

Have you ever seen a shepherd tending his flock? He is either in front of the sheep or behind them if it is a regular grazing site. The sheep know his voice, and wherever he commands them to go that is where they go. If there are any disobedient sheep, the shepherd will hit them lightly to make them obey, and walk with the rest of the flock. When I was growing up, my image of Jesus was that of the Good Shepherd, because of the portrait of the Good Shepherd that hung in our sitting room. We learned and recited Psalm 23 by heart. Whenever we prayed this psalm, my mum would point to the portrait of the Good Shepherd and narrate to us how the lamb that Jesus was carrying on his right arm was each of us. From her stories we learned as children that Jesus cares for us.

Jesus uses the metaphor of sheep and shepherd in communicating his love for us. For the Jews, one of their images of God is God as the Shepherd of Israel (Ps 80:1). This metaphor is presented as a result of Jesus' healing of the man born blind, despite it being the Sabbath. This healing incurs the wrath of the Pharisees since Jesus has broken the Sabbath law. Jesus tells them that he is the Good Shepherd because he cares for his sheep even on a Sabbath. He knows the sheep by name, he heals them, and he leads them to the path of life. The way that Jesus talks about being a Good Shepherd, implies that there are also bad shepherds. In Ezekiel 34:1-10, God through Ezekiel prophesied against the shepherds who did not feed the sheep, strengthen the weak, or bring back those that had strayed, but allowed them to be scattered and become prey for wild animals. Being good to the sheep is a selfless and noble work, and it involves caring for their needs—spiritually and materially. Jesus as a Shepherd did not only sacrifice his life for the sheep, but he also protected them from harm. The shepherding of Jesus is different from a hired worker, who works on a contract basis but does not necessarily care for the sheep as his own. The hired worker cannot sacrifice his life for the sheep because he does not own them, and because there is no relationship between him and the flock. On the other hand, Jesus is tender to his sheep and loves them even with the love that he has for his Father.

I read on the internet how in Australia a man was accused of stealing a sheep. When he was brought before the court, the judge did not know how to decide the case. He ordered the plaintiff to call the sheep in, but the sheep was scared to enter. Then he asked the defendant or the accused to call the sheep in, and immediately the sheep entered the courtroom. The case was dismissed since it was obvious that the sheep had recognized the voice of its owner.

Jesus knows us well, do we really know him, and do we listen to his voice when he calls? Do we also help our stray brothers and sisters to find the Good Shepherd? Jesus laid down his life so that we might have life abundantly. He also reconciles us with his Father through his death so that we may participate in the Triune relational love. The Good Shepherd is carrying us tenderly and lovingly in his arms just as the portrait of the Shepherd we are familiar with. The question is: Do we recognize his voice? The case in Australia was in favor of the owner because the sheep recognized the owner's voice. Do we recognize the voice of the Good Shepherd? When he calls us, do we follow him?

CONCLUSION

"Immense are the desires that I feel within my heart, and it is with confidence that I call upon Thee to come and take possession of my soul."

—St. Thérèse of Lisieux (*Story of a Soul*)

"Out of the Lips of Infants, Wisdom Comes." How true is this statement? Have you ever pondered on the innocence, sincerity and child-like wisdom that kids exude? The story of the wooden bowl will illustrate my point.

A frail old man went to live with his son, daughter-in-law, and four- year-old grandson. The old man's hands trembled, his eyesight was blurred, and his step faltered. The family ate together at the table, but the elderly grandfather's shaky hands and failing sight made eating difficult. Peas rolled off his spoon onto the floor. When he grasped the glass, milk spilled on the tablecloth. The son and daughter-in-law became irritated with the mess. "We must do something about father," said the son. "I've had enough of his spilled milk, noisy eating, and food on the floor." Emphatically, his wife agreed.

So, the husband and wife set a small table at the corner. There, grandfather ate alone while the rest of the family enjoyed dinner at their dining table. Since grandfather had broken a dish or two, his food was served in a wooden bowl. When the family glanced in grandfather's direction, sometimes he had a tear in his eye as he sat alone. Still, the only words the couple had for him were sharp admonitions when he dropped a fork or spilled food on the floor.

Their four-year-old child watched all this in silence. One evening before supper, the father noticed his son playing with wood scraps on the floor. He asked the child sweetly, "What are you making son?" Just as sweetly, the boy responded: "Oh, I am making a little bowl for you and mum to eat your food from when I grow up." The child smiled and went back to work. His parents were speechless, and then tears started to stream down their cheeks. Although no word was spoken, the little boy's parents knew what they had to do.

That evening, the husband took the grandfather's hand and gently led him back to the family table. For the remainder of his days, he ate every meal with the family. After that neither husband nor wife seemed to care any longer when a fork was dropped, milk spilled, or the tablecloth soiled.[1]

Children are very wise and we need only to listen attentively to them. At the introduction of this book, I told a story about my nephew Vincent, but left out the end of it. Now it's time for the rest. Vincent understood that losing his limbs would not make him less human, so I went a step further to find out how much he knew about being human and being created in God's image. "When you die what happens?" I asked him. "My soul leaves the body!" he replied. "So, which one is you at that phase in your life, your soul or your lifeless body or both?" I probed. He looked at me as if to ask: "Can't Auntie see the obvious answer to her question?" "My soul," he emphasized. I then drove home the message, "Go measure your imaginary Soul-self!" On hearing the final test—measuring his soul— which is mathematically impossible, he protested in surrender, "Auntie, I can't." I

---

[1] https://www.moralstories.org/the-wooden-bowl/

asked him why he thought he couldn't, and I was pleasantly surprised when he was able to grasp the concept of his soul being more
like the image of God, a spirit, and therefore immeasurable and im-
mortal.

If our souls are like God—immeasurable, unlimited, and infinite—then the physical body and the activities that serve its suste-
nance should ultimately highlight and mirror the likeness of God.
Children, in their own rudimentary way, readily and genuinely believe and trust in God, just as they trust in their care-givers. These
young minds mirror for us how to completely depend and trust in
God. Their lips are filled with wisdom.

Jesus is the Wisdom of God (1 Cor. 1:24) and the Word of God
(Jn. 1:1, 14), he finds it fitting to share his wisdom with mere infants
(Mt. 11:25). This work has tried to reflect on the Word of God with
stories and parables. As the Word is proclaimed to us, may we embrace it for what it really is: the Word of God (1 Thes. 2:13) and allow
it to bear fruit in our life, even if it is from a mere infant.

EPILOGUE

"BUT WE HAD HOPED…" THE JOURNEY WITH JESUS DURING THE COVID-19 PANDEMIC

"In times of aridity when I am incapable of praying, I seek little opportunities to give pleasure to Jesus; for instance a smile or a pleasant word. If I find no opportunities, I at least tell Him again and again that I love Him."

—St. Thérèse of Lisieux (XVI letter to her Sister Celine)

The imagined silence of God was felt during the outbreak of Coronavirus pandemic in the year 2020 and beyond. We were scared and disillusioned. It felt like walking in a lonely desert and feeling the absence of God. The clouds were gloomy and bleak. The number of deaths were increasing daily. The healthcare providers and first responders, who are at the front line of the COVID-19 outbreak response, were overwhelmed because of pathogen exposure, long working hours, psychological distress and trauma, fatigue, and occupational burnout. The entire world was at a standstill. The world was filled with fear, just as were the disciples on the way to Emmaus (Lk. 24:12-32).

"We had hoped…" But the hope was dashed to the ground. In their misery, dejection, helplessness and fear, they were not able to see beyond those feelings. The One they had hoped would save them walked beside them, but in their clouded mind, they called him a Stranger. The Stranger understood their predicaments and handled them with tenderness and patience. Even though they continued oblivious to his message, he began teaching them again, right from the beginning: the Torah of Moses, the Prophets, actually the entire Hebrew Scriptures. When their eyes were opened at the Breaking of the Bread, the Stranger became the One that they "had hoped."

God meets us where we are and gives us what we need to stay calm, even when we imagine Him to be silent. Jesus is offering to journey with us, and he offers us His love during the outbreak of this Coronavirus pandemic: when our churches were shut down for months; when neighbors are not visiting neighbors; when we are to maintain social distancing and wear face masks in public places.

In the midst of our fears, Jesus tells us: "Be not afraid, I am with you on the journey. This darkness will pass away. These clouds will clear and better days will come." If the mountains are smooth, no one would climb them! The world is not a bed of roses. Even if it were, then the thorns that surround the roses would welcome the body that decided to sleep on this bed. No matter how much darkness covers the earth, the sun will always rise up at dawn and shower us with sunshine. Jesus is the Sun that never sets; the true Light that shines in our darkened world! Stay with us Lord Jesus!

REFERENCES

Abogunrin, Samuel Oyin."Luke." In *The International Bible Commentary*, edited by William Farmer, et al., 1368-1437. Collegeville, MN: The Liturgical Press, 1998.

Adams, Joanna. "Faith and Fear: 1 John 4:16-19 and Matthew 14:22-33." *Journal for Preachers* 19, no. 4 (Pentecost 1996): 25-29.

Andolsen, Barbara. "Whose Sexuality? Whose Tradition? Women, Experience, and Roman Catholic Sexual Ethics." In *Feminist Ethics and the Catholic Moral Tradition*, edited by Charles Curran, Margaret Farley, and Richard McCormick, 207-239. New York, NY: Paulist Press, 1996.

Aquinas, Thomas. *Commentary on the Gospel of John: Chapter 13-21*. Translated by Fabian Larcher and James Weisheipl. Washington, DC: The Catholic University of America Press, 2010.

Aquinas, Thomas. *The Summa Theologica of St. Thomas Aquinas*, Vol. 1. New York: Benziger Brothers Inc., 1947.

Bailey, Jon Nelson. "Looking for Luke's Fingerprints: Identifying Evidence of Redactional Activity in 'The Healing of the Paralytic' (Luke 5:17-26)." *Restoration Quarterly* 48, no. 3 (2006):143-156.

Bakhos, Carol. "Post-Biblical Interpretation." In *The Torah: A Women's Commentary*, edited by Tamara C. Eskenazi and Andrea Weiss, 150-151. New York, NY: Women of Reform Judaism Press, 2008.

Bergant Dianne and Fragomeni Richard. *Preaching the New Lectionary: Year A*. Collegeville, MN: Liturgical Press, 2001.

Bergant Dianne and Fragomeni Richard. *Preaching the New Lectionary: Year B.* Collegeville, MN: Liturgical Press, 2001.

Bergant Dianne and Fragomeni Richard. *Preaching the New Lectionary: Year C.* Collegeville, MN: Liturgical Press, 2001.

Berner, Douglas. *The Silence is Broken! God Hooks Ezekiel's Gog and Magog.* Morrisville, NC: Lulu Press, 2006.

Boring, Eugene. "The Gospel of Matthew: Introduction, Commentary, and Reflections." In *The New Interpreter's Bible*, Vol. VIII, edited by Leander Keck et al., 87-506. Nashville, TN: Abingdon Press, 1995.

Brueggemann, Walter. "From Hurt to Joy, from Death to Life." *Interpretation* 28, no. 1 (Jan. 1974): 3-19.

Brueggemann, Walter. *The Message of the Psalms: A Theological Commentary.* Minneapolis, MN: Augsburg Publishing House, 1984.

Brueggemann, Walter. "Psalms and the Life of Faith: A Suggested Typology of Function." *Journal for the Study of the Old Testament*, no. 17 (Je 1980): 3-32.

Brueggemann, Walter. "Voice as Counter to Violence." *Calvin Theological Journal* 36, no. 1 (April 2001): 22-33.

Bruner, Frederick. *Matthew: A Commentary. Vol. 2, revised and expanded edition.* Grand Rapids, MI: William B. Eerdmans, 2004.

Button-Harrison, Tim. "Walking on Water: Mark 4:35-41, Matthew 14:22-32." *Brethren Life and Thought* 52, no. 4 (Fall 2007): 244-247.

Byrne, Brendan. *Romans. Sacra Pagina Series, Vol. 6,* edited by Daniel Harrington. Collegeville, MN: The Liturgical Press, 1996.

Champlin, Joseph, and Peter Jarret. *Together For Life: Celebrating and Living the Sacrament*. 5th ed. Notre Dame, IN: Ave Maria Press, 2012.

Chinchar, Gerald, Paul Colloton, and Roc O'Connor. "Praying the Psalms in the Light of the Paschal Mystery." *Liturgical Ministry*, no. 16 (Winter 2007): 53-59.

Chung, Sook Ja. "Women's Ways of Doing Mission in the Story of Mary and Martha." *International Review of Mission* 93, no. 368 (Jan 2004): 9-16.

Clifford, Richard. "Genesis 27:19-34." *Interpretation* 45, no. 4 (October 1991): 397-401.

Cobb, John, and David Lull. Romans. *Chalice Commentaries for Today*. St. Louis, MO: Chalice Press, 2005.

Cohen, Norman. "Two That Are One: Sibling Rivalry in Genesis." *Judaism* 32, no. 3 (Sum 1983): 331-342.

Corbett, Lionel. *The Religious Functions of the Psyche*. New York, NY: Routledge, 1996.

Crenshaw, James L. *The Psalms: An Introduction*. Grand Rapids, MI: William B Eerdmans Publishing Company, 2001.

Culpepper, Alan. "The Gospel of Luke." In *The New Interpreter's Bible*, Vol. IX, edited by Leander Keck, et al., 1-490. Nashville, TN: Abingdon Press, 1995.

D'Angelo, Mary Rose. "Mary 2." In *Women in Scripture: A Dictionary of Named and Unnamed Women in the Hebrew Bible, The Apocryphal/ Deuterocanonical Books and The New Testament*, edited by Carol Meyers, Toni Craven, and Ross Kraemer,119-120. Grand Rapids, MI: Wm. B. Eerdmans Publishers, 2001.

Davidson, Robert. *The Vitality of Worship: A Commentary on the Book of Psalms.* Grand Rapids, MI: William B. Eerdmans Publishers, 1998.

Davies, W. D. and Allison Dale. *Matthew: A Shorter Commentary.* Edited by Allison Dale. New York, NY: T and T Clark International, 2004.

Deardorn, Kerry. "Matthew." In *The IVP Women's Bible Commentary,* edited by Catherine and Kroeger and Mary Evans, 517-546. Downers Grove, IL: Intervarsity Press, 2002.

Donahue, John and Harrington Daniel. "Gospel of Mark." In *Sacra Pagina Series,* Edited by Daniel Harrington. Collegeville, MN: The Liturgical Press, 1991.

Dufner, Delores, "With What Language Will We Pray?" *Worship* 80, no. 2 (March 2006): 140-161.

Eaton, John. *The Psalms: A Historical and Spiritual Commentary with an Introduction and New Translation.* New York, NY: The Continuum International Publishers, 2005.

Elazar, J. Daniel. "Jacob and Esau and the Emergence of the Jewish People." *Judaism* 43, no. 3 (Summer 1994): 294-301.

Eskenazi, Tamara, and Hara Person. "Shaping Destiny: The Story of Rebekah." In *The Torah: A Women's Commentary,* edited by Tamara C. Eskenazi and Andrea Weiss, 133-149. New York, NY: Women of Reform Judaism Press, 2008.

Fallon, Michael. *The Gospel According to Matthew: An Introduction Commentary.* Bangalore, India: Asian Trading Corporation, 2002.

Farley, Margaret. *Just Love: A Framework for Christian Sexual Ethics.* New York, NY: The Continuum International Publishers, 2006.

Farmer, Kathleen A. "Psalms." In *Women's Bible Commentary, Expanded Edition with Apocrypha,* edited by Carol A. Newsom and Sharon H. Ringe. Original print 1992, Louisville, KY: Westminster John Knox Press, 1998.

Fitzmyer, Joseph. *Paul and His Theology: A Brief Sketch.* 2nd ed. Englewood Cliffs, NJ: Prentice Hall, 1989.

Fitzmyer, Joseph. "Pauline Theology." In *The New Jerome Biblical Commentary,* edited by Raymond Brown, Joseph Fitzmyer, and Roland Murphy, 1382-1416. Englewood Cliffs, NJ: Prentice Hall, 1990.

Fitzmyer, Joseph. "The Letter to the Romans." In *The New Jerome Biblical Commentary,* edited by Raymond Brown, Joseph Fitzmyer, and Roland Murphy, 830-868. Englewood Cliffs, NJ: Prentice Hall, 1990.

Forbes, Christopher. "Paul and Rhetorical Comparison." In *Paul in the Greco-Roman World: A Handbook,* edited by J. Paul Sampley, 134-171. Harrisburg, PA: Trinity Press, 2003.

Gaiser, Frederick. "Come and See What God Has Done": The Psalms of Easter." *Word and World* 7, no. 2 (1987): 207-214.

Gaiser, Frederick. "I Will Tell You What God Has Done for Me" (Psalm 66:16): A Place of "Testimony" in Lutheran Worship?" *Word and World* 26, no. 2 (Spring 2006):138-148.

Gillman, John. *Luke: Stories of Joy and Salvation.* Edited by Mary Ann Getty-Sullivan. Hyde Park, NY: New City Press, 2002.

Goodnick, Benjamin. "Rebekah's Deceit or Isaac's Great Test." *The Jewish Bible Quarterly* 23, no. 4 (October-December 1995): 221-228.

Graves, Mike. "Followed by the Sun: Matthew 14:22-33." *Review and Expositor* 99, no. 1 (Winter 2002): 91-96.

Guinan, Michael D. "'They Cried to the Lord!' Lamentinthe Bible," Posted by Update Your Faith, Feb. 2004, http://www.american-catholic.org/ Newsletters/SFS/an0204.asp (accessed 24th March, 2009).

Haacker, Klaus. *New Testament Theology: The Theology of Paul's Letter to the Romans.* New York, NY: Cambridge University Press, 2003.

Halton, Thomas et al., eds. *St. Jerome Commentary on Matthew, a new translation,* Vol. 117. Translated by Thomas Scheck. Washington, DC: The Catholic University of America Press, 2008.

Harrington, Daniel. "The Gospel of Matthew." In *Sacra Pagina Series,* Vol. 1. Edited by DanielHarrington. Collegeville, MN: The Liturgical Press, 1991.

Hawkins, Peter. "Dogging Jesus." *Christian Century* 122, no.16 (August 2005): 18.

Johnson, Luke T. *The Gospel of Luke. Sacra Pagina,* Vol. 3. Edited by Daniel Harrington. Collegeville, MN: The Liturgical Press, 1991.

Kalt, Edmund. *Herder's Commentary on the Psalms.* Westminster, Maryland: The Newman Press, 1961.

Kapolyo, Joe. "Matthew." In *African Bible Commentary,* edited by Tokunboh Adeyemo et al., 1105-1170. Nairobi, Kenya: Wordalive Publishers, 2006.

Karris, Robert. "The Gospel According to Luke." In *The New Jerome Biblical Commentary*, edited by Raymond Brown, Joseph Fitzmyer, and Roland Murphy, 675-721. Englewood Cliffs, NJ: Prentice Hall, 1990.

Kasali, David. "Romans." In *African Bible Commentary*, edited by Tokunboh Adeyemo,1349-1376. Nairobi, Kenya: WordAlive Publishers, 2006.

Kinzer, Mark. *Post-Missionary Messianic Judaism: Redefining Christian Engagement with the Jewish People*. Grand Rapids, MI: Brazos Press, 2005.

Knight, G. A. F. *Psalms Volume 1*. Philadelphia, PA: The Westminster Press, 1982.

König, Adrio. "Gentiles or Gentile Christians? On the Meaning of Romans 2:12-16." *Journal of Theology for Southern Africa*, no. 15 (January 1976): 53-60.

Kraus, Hans-Joachim. *Psalms 60-150: A Commentary*. Translated by Hilton Oswald. Minneapolis, MN: Augsburg Fortress, 1989.

Kraus, Hans Joachim. *Theology of the Psalms*. Minneapolis, MN: Augsburg Publishing House, 1986.

Krentz, Edgar. "The Name of God in Disrepute: Romans 2:17-29." *Currents in Theology and Mission* 17, no.6 (December 1990): 429-439.

Kselman, John, and Michael Barré. "Psalms." In *The New Jerome Biblical Commentary*, edited by Raymond Brown, Joseph Fitzmyer, and Roland Murphy, 523-552. Englewood Cliffs, NJ: Prentice Hall, 1990.

Kurek-Chomycz, Dominika K. "The Fragrance of Her Perfume: The Significance of Sense Imagery in John's Account of the Anointing in Bethany." *Novum Testamentum* 52, (2010): 334-354.

Laki, Stanley. *Praying the Psalms: A Commentary.* Grand Rapids, MI: William B. Eerdmans Publishing Company, 2001.

Lamp, Jeffery. "Paul, the Law, Jews, and Gentiles: A Contextual and Exegetical Reading of Romans 2:12-16." *Journal of the Evangelical Theological Society* 42, no.1 (March 1999): 37-51.

Leonard, Richard C. "Praying the Psalms of Imprecation," Posted by Laudemont Ministries, Jan 1, 2005, http://www.laudemont.org/a-ptsoi.htm (accessed 24th March, 2009).

Leske, Adrian. "Matthew." In *The International Bible Commentary: A Catholic and Ecumenical Commentary for the Twenty-First Century,* edited by William Farmer et al., 1253-1330. Collegeville, MN: The Liturgical Press, 1998.

Levenson, Jon. "Genesis: Introduction and Annotations." In *The Jewish Study Bible,* edited by Adele Berlin and Marc Z. Brettler, 8-101. New York, NY: Oxford University Press, 2004.

Levine, Amy-Jill, "Matthew." In *Women's Bible Commentary, Expanded Edition with Apocrypha,* edited by Carol Newsom and Sharon Ringe, 339-349. Louisville, KY: Westminster John Knox Press, 1998.

Lieber, Valerie. "Contemporary Reflection." In *The Torah: A Women's Commentary,* edited by Tamara C. Eskenazi and Andrea Weiss, 152-153. New York, NY: Women of Reform Judaism Press, 2008.

Limburg, James. *Psalms.* Edited by Patrick Miller and David Bartlett. Louisville, KY: Westminster John Knox Press, 2000.

John Paul II. *"Salvifici Doloris," Christian Meaning of Human Suffer-ing*, Catholic Information Network, http://www.cin.org/suf-fer.html (accessed May 6, 2012).

Make Straight Paths. "Praying Against Enemies," Posted 2006, (Anonymous author), http://makestraightpaths.com/praying_against_enemies.htm (accessed 24th March, 2009).

Malina, Bruce, and Richard Rohrbaugh. *Social-Science Commentary on the Gospel of John*. Minneapolis, MN: Augsburg Press, 1998.

Martin, Scott. "Matthew 15:21-28: A Test-Case for Jesus' Manners." Journal for the Study of theNew Testament, no. 63 (September 1996): 21-44.

McKenna, Megan. *Prophets: Words of Fire*. Maryknoll, NY: Orbis Books, 2001.

Matthew, Henry and Thomas Scott. *Commentary on the Holy Bible: Job-Malachi*. Nashville, TN: Thomas Nelson Inc. Publishers, 1979.

McCann, Clinton J. "The Book of Psalms: Introduction, Commen-tary and Reflections." In *The New Interpreter's Bible Vol. IV*, ed-ited by Leander E. Keck et al. Nashville, TN: Abingdon Press, 1996.

McCullough, Stewart W. *The Interpreter's Bible, Vol. IV*. Edited by George Buttrick, et al. Nashville, TN: Abingdon Press, 1955.

Moloney, Francis. "The Gospel of John" In *Sacra Pagina Series, Vol. 4*, Edited by Daniel Harrington. Collegeville, MN: The Liturgical Press, 1998.

Mowinckel, Sigmund. *The Psalms in Israel's Worship*. Grand Rapids, MI: William B. Eerdmans Publishing Company, 2004.

Murphy-O'Connor, Jerome. *Paul: A Critical Life*. Oxford, NY: Oxford University Press, 1996.

Ngewa, Samuel. "John." In *African Bible Commentary*, edited by Tokunboh Adeyemo et. al, 1251-1296. Nairobi, Kenya: WordAlive Publishers, 2006.

Nissen, Johannes. "Matthew, Mission, and Method." *International Review of Mission* 91, no. 360 (January 2002): 73-86.

Nolland, John. "'Have Mercy on Me': The Story of the Canaanite Woman in Matthew 15:21-28." *Journal of Theological Studies* 55, no.1 (April 2004): 234-236.

O'Day, Gail. "John." In *Women's Bible Commentary*, edited by Carol Newson and Sharon Ringe, 381-393. Louisville, KY: Westminster John Knox Press, 1998.

Oduyoye, Mercy. *Introducing African Women's Theology*. Cleveland, OH: The Pilgrim Press, 2001.

Ogbuji, Adaku Helen. *Dealing Effectively with Domestic Abuse: The Ministry of Reconciliation and Healing*. Nairobi, Kenya: CUEA Press, 2015.

Okure Teresa. "Luke." In *The International Bible Commentary*, edited by William Farmer, et al., Collegeville, MN: The Liturgical Press, 1998.

Ortberg, John. *Love Beyond Reason: Moving God's Love from Your Head to Your Heart*. Grand Rapids, MI: Zondervan Publishing House 1998.

Oyediran, Kolawole, and Uche Isiugo-Abanihe. "Perceptions of Nigerian Women on Domestic Violence: Evidence from 2003

Nigeria Demographic and Health Survey." *African Journal of Reproductive Health* 9, no. 2 (August 2005): 38-53.

Pazdan, Mary Margaret. *Becoming God's Beloved in the Company of Friends: A Spirituality of the Fourth Gospel.* Eugene, OR: Cascade Books, 2007.

Perkins, Pheme. "The Gospel According to John." In *The New Jerome Biblical Commentary*, edited by Raymond Brown, Joseph Fitzmyer, and Roland Murphy, 942-985. Englewood Cliffs, NY: 1990.

Phelps, Stephen. "Luke 13:10-17." *Interpretation* 55, no.1 (January 2001): 64-66.

Plaut, W. Gunther, Bernard Bamberger, and William Hallo. *The Torah: A Modern Commentary.* New York, NY: The Union of American Hebrew Congregations, 1981.

Pope Paul VI. "Apostolic Constitution Promulgation, The Divine Office" (Nov.1, 1970), Sec 4, *Christian Prayer: The Liturgy of the Hours.* Boston: Daughters of St. Paul Publication, 1976.

Porter, Calvin. "God's Justice and the Culture of the Law: Conflicting Traditions in Paul's Letter to the Romans." *Encounter* 59, no. 1-2 (Spring 1998): 135-155.

Pregeant, Russell. *Matthew: Chalice Commentaries for Today.* St. Louis, MO: Chalice Press, 2004.

Puskas, Charles. *The Letters of Paul: An Introduction.* Collegeville, MN: The Liturgical Press, 1993.

Räisänen, Heikki. *Paul and the Law.* Philadelphia, PA: Fortress Press, 1986.

Reid, Barbara. "Sabbath, the Crown of Creation." In *Earth, Wind, and Fire: Biblical and Theological Perspectives on Creation*, edited by Carol Dempsey and Mary Margaret Pazdan, 67-76. Collegeville, MN: Liturgical Press, 2004.

Reinhartz, Adele. "Women in the Johannine Community: An Exercise in Historical Imagination." In *A Feminist Companion to John, Volume II,* edited by Amy-Jill Levine and Marianne Blickenstaff, 14-33. New York, NY: Sheffield Academic Press, 2003.

Saint Thérèse of Lisieux. *Story of a Soul: The Autobiography of St. Thérèse of Lisieux,* 3rd Edition. Translated by John Clarke. Washington, D.C: ICS Publications, 1996.

Schaefer, Konrad. *Psalms: Studies in Hebrew Narrative and Poetry.* Edited by David Cotter, et al. Collegeville, MN: The Liturgical Press, 2001.

Schindler, Pesach. "Esau and Jacob Revisited: Demon versus Tzadik?" *Jewish Bible Quarterly* 35, no.3 (2007): 153-160.

Schnackenburg, Rudolf. *The Gospel of Matthew.* Translated by Robert Barr. Grand Rapids, MI: William B. Eerdmans Company, 2002.

Schneiders, Sandra. *Written That You May Believe: Encountering Jesus in the Fourth Gospel.* 2nd ed. New York, NY: Herder and Herder, 2003.

Shannon, Martin. "A Certain Psychological Difficulty or A Certain Spiritual Challenge: Use of The Integral Psalter in the Liturgy of the Hours." *Worship* 73, no. 4 (July 1999): 290-309.

Smith, Barry D. "The Letter to the Romans: The New Testament and Its Context." Crandall University (August 6, 2008). http://www.abu.nb.ca/courses/ntintro/ Rom.htm (accessed October 10, 2010).

Spero, Shubert. "Jacob and Esau: The Relationship Reconsidered." *Jewish Bible Quarterly* 32, no. 4 (2004): 245-250.

Stone, Howard. *Theological Context for Pastoral Caregiving: Word in Deed*. Binghamton, NY: The Haworth Pastoral Press, 1996.

Stuhlmueller, Carroll. *The Spirituality of the Psalms*. Collegeville, MN: The Liturgical Press, 2002.

Travers, Michael E. *Encountering God in the Psalms*. Grand Rapids, MI: Kregel Publications, 2003.

Torgerson, Heidi. "The Healing of the Bent Woman: A Narrative Interpretation of Luke 13:10-17." *Currents in Theology and Mission* 32, no. 3 (January 2005):176-186.

Turner, Mary Donovan. "Rebekah: Ancestor of Faith." *Lexington Theological Quarterly* 20, no. 2 (April 1985): 42-50.

Viviano Benedict. "The Gospel According to Matthew." In *The New Jerome Biblical Commentary*. Edited by Raymond Brown, Joseph Fitzmyer, and Roland Murphy. Englewood Cliffs, NJ: Prentice Hall, 1990.

Watson, Duane. "Paul and Boasting." In *Paul in the Greco-Roman World: A Handbook*, edited by J. Paul Sampley, 77-100. Harrisburg, PA: Trinity Press, 2003.

Westermann, Claus. *The Living Psalms*. Grand Rapids, MI: William B. Eerdmans Publishing Company, 1989.

Witherington, Ben, and Darlene Hyatt. *Paul's Letter to the Romans: A Socio-Rhetorical Commentary*. Grand Rapids, MI: William B. Eerdmans Publishers, 2004.

Wright, N.T. "The Letter to the Romans." In *The New Interpreter's Bible*, Vol. X, edited by Leander Keck et al, 393-770. Nashville, TN: Abingdon Press, 2002.

Zucker, David. "The Deceiver Deceived: Rereading Genesis 27." *Jewish Bible Quarterly* 39, no.1 (2011): 46-58.

www.ingramcontent.com/pod-product-compliance
Lightning Source LLC
Chambersburg PA
CBHW051417090426
42737CB00014B/2707